SHAPESHIFTERS

© Shane Van Boxtel

About the Author

Nick Redfern is the author of more than thirty books on the worlds of the paranormal, the supernatural, and the unknown. His previous titles include *Chupacabra Road Trip*, *Nessie*, and *Men in Black*. Nick has appeared on dozens of television shows, including SyFy Channel's *Proof Positive*, History Channel's *Monster Quest*, Nat Geo Wild's *The Monster Project*, and Fox News. He lives just a short drive from the infamous Grassy Knoll of Dallas, Texas. Nick can be contacted at his blog, *World of Whatever*: http://nickredfernfortean.blogspot.com.

SHAPESHIFTERS

MORPHING MONSTERS
& CHANGING CRYPTIDS

NICK REDFERN

Llewellyn Publications
Woodbury, Minnesota

FIRST EDITION
First Printing, 2017

Cover design: Kevin R. Brown
Cover illustration: Dominick Finelle / July Group
Interior photos provided by the author

Llewellyn Publications is a registered trademark of Llewellyn Worldwide Ltd.

Library of Congress Cataloging-in-Publication Data (Pending)
ISBN: 978-0-7387-5203-7

Llewellyn Worldwide Ltd. does not participate in, endorse, or have any authority or responsibility concerning private business transactions between our authors and the public.

All mail addressed to the author is forwarded but the publisher cannot, unless specifically instructed by the author, give out an address or phone number.

Any Internet references contained in this work are current at publication time, but the publisher cannot guarantee that a specific location will continue to be maintained. Please refer to the publisher's website for links to authors' websites and other sources.

Llewellyn Publications
A Division of Llewellyn Worldwide Ltd.
2143 Wooddale Drive
Woodbury, MN 55125-2989
www.llewellyn.com

Printed in the United States of America

Other Books by Nick Redfern

The Bigfoot Book
Chupacabra Road Trip
Men in Black
Nessie
Women in Black

Contents

INTRODUCTION

THE BOOK THAT YOU are about to read deals with a subject that many people might assume falls solely into the domains of folklore, mythology, and legend. They would, however, be wrong. In fact, they would be *acutely* wrong. Shapeshifting, for most people, provokes imagery of nothing more than centuries-old tales of savage, murderous werewolves and of big-bucks movies, such as *An American Werewolf in London*, *Underworld*, *Dog Soldiers*, and *The Wolfman*. That is not the case, however. As incredible as it may seem, shapeshifters are not merely the stuff of Hollywood and urban tales of the friend-of-a-friend variety. Rather, they are all too menacingly real. And, they are not all of the man-turns-into-wolf variety, either. Quite the opposite, actually: shapeshifters come in all kinds and sizes and have done so for countless millennia.

While the traditional image of the werewolf is, without a doubt, the first thing that springs to mind when a discussion of shapeshifters takes place, the truth of the matter is that there is a veritable menagerie of such infernal things in our midst. Were-cats, were-tigers, were-hyenas, and were-coyotes are also near the top of the monstrous list. Then, there are the ancient beliefs that those who died violent deaths—or those who were, themselves, murderers—were often destined to return to our plain of existence in the forms of hideous beasts, including wild and savage ape-like animals, fearsome black dogs with glowing and blazing red eyes, and mermaid-like things. There are also beings from other worlds: aliens, extraterrestrials, and Men in Black.

Even the legendary monsters of Loch Ness, in Scotland, are believed—in certain monster-hunting quarters—to be paranormal beasts that have the ability to alter their appearances at will. As are legendary vampires, who, the old legends suggest, can transform into the likes of bats and wolves.

Collectively, all of these "things" amount to an absolute army of otherworldly creatures and half-human monsters that have plagued and tormented us since the dawning of civilization. And, they show zero signs of slowing down anytime soon. The things you thought were only fit for campfire tales, late-night stories intended to thrill little children, and entertaining monster-movies are, in actuality, creatures of the real world. Of our world. Shapeshifters are everywhere: they lurk in the shadows, in the deep woods and expansive forests, in dark and dank caves, and in the murky waters of our lakes and rivers. Maybe even, after sunset, in the recesses of your very own backyard, patiently waiting to pounce. And many of them like nothing better than to terrorize and torment us, the human race.

With that all said, it's now time to take a wild and weird road-trip into the mystery-filled domain of creatures that so many will assure you simply do not exist. I'm here, however, to tell you otherwise. Shapeshifters are disturbingly real. And you're about to meet them, in all their savage and sinister glory.

As you read *Shapeshifters*, and as day becomes night, keep those silver bullets close at hand. *Very* close. You know, just in case …

1
WEREWOLVES OF THE PAST

TAKING INTO CONSIDERATION THE subject matter of this book, it's only appropriate that we start with the world's most famous shape-shifter of them all, the werewolf. A full moon and monstrous mayhem are part and parcel of both legend and reality when it comes to this particular breed of supernatural monster.

There is no doubt that many of the centuries-old reports of werewolves originated specifically in Europe. One person with a particular interest in such tales was Alexander Schöppner. In the latter part of the nineteenth century he published a fascinating tale that fits right into the pages of this book. It was in 1874 when the story surfaced, in the pages of Schöppner's book *The Legend of the Bavarian Lands: From the Mouths of the People, the Chronicles, and the Poets*; however, it told a story that dated back centuries. The location was Bavaria, Germany, and specifically the Fichtel Mountains, which cover Germany's Red Main River to the border of the Czech Republic.

So Schöppner's story went, the mystery began when a local shepherd realized that day by day his flock of sheep was growing smaller and smaller. Something deadly and predatory was on the loose. But what? That was the big question the shepherd wanted answering—and before he lost anymore of his flock.

Finally, there was an answer: the shepherd caught sight of a massive wolf that emerged from the nearby woods and seized and killed one of his baby lambs. He knew all too well that the wolf was clearly not going to stop, and regular attacks and killings were likely to continue. Unless, that is, the shepherd decided to take matters into his own hands—which he did.

The man was acquainted with a particular character who was an expert shooter. When the shepherd asked for his help in killing the creature, he eagerly agreed. It was not quite the easy situation that both may have anticipated. When the wolf finally made its next appearance, the hunter carefully aimed his gun and fired. That is when things got very strange: the bullet quite literally bounced off the body of the massive, muscular animal. The hunter was not going to give up that easily, however.

On the very next day, shepherd and shooter were back again—lying in wait for the monster-wolf. This time, the shot not only hit the animal but wounded it, to the point that it raced back into the thick trees from which it had first surfaced. Then, things got even weirder. On the next day, he ran into another villager—an old woman whom he had crossed paths with previously, and not in a positive or good way. He noticed something as they crossed paths: she was noticeably limping. The possibility that the woman and the beast were one and the same quickly crossed the man's mind.

Scowling at him, she effectively told the man to mind his own business. He remained convinced that something strange was going down, chiefly because the old woman had, for a long time, been suspected of practicing the black arts. And, although nothing was ever conclusively proved, suspicions still remained that she was guilty of the attacks—and particularly so when she managed to escape from a nearby jail after being briefly incarcerated on suspicion of being the culprit. There was far more to come.

On the next occasion, long after the sun had set, the wolf was back. This time, however, the beast was not seeking out a sheep or a lamb. No—it was set upon feeding on human flesh. The farmer's flesh. The monster lunged at the man, and a wild battle to the death began. While the wolf certainly had the upper hand—or the upper paw, to be correct—it was most fortunate for the man that his hunter friend was soon on the scene and not only shot the beast but plunged his knife into it, too. Then something dramatic occurred: the wolf, as it lay dying, started to transform into the old witch. The horrified pair sped up the dying process and buried her body deep below the ground. So the story went, a cross was placed over the burial site, which became known locally as the Wolf Stone. According to Schöppner, from then on the specific patch of land was perceived as evil.

A Fearsome Family

The latter part of the 1800s saw yet another mysterious tale of shape-shifting surface out of Germany—a country that has a long and checkered history of encounters with werewolves. It's specifically to the year of 1879 and the town of Ludwigslust to which we have to turn our attentions; it is a town with origins that date back to 1724, when one Prince Ludwig—also known as Christian Ludwig II— had his workers construct a hunting lodge in the area. Such was the prince's love of the area that he renamed it Ludwigslust. Today, the town is dominated by the huge Ludwigslust Palace. In 1879, however, the area was dominated by werewolves, a family of them.

Even more than a century after the prince's passing in 1756, the area was still a favorite one for hunting wild animals. One particular creature that became almost legendary was a large, wild wolf that seemingly was completely unaffected by bullets. The brazen beast would even creep up on hunters and steal their bounty— their dinner, in other words. It's no surprise that word soon got around that maybe the wolf was more than just a nimble animal that had been lucky enough to avoid getting shot. Some thought it was supernatural in nature. Others, in quiet tones, suggested Ludwigslust had its very own werewolf. They were right.

On one particular day, a cavalryman rode into town atop his horse with the intention of meeting a man who history only records as Feeg. The military officer found Feeg's isolated home quickly. But he didn't find Feeg. Instead, he was confronted by a terrified group of young children who were seemingly fleeing for their lives, amid hysterical cries for help. One of the group breathlessly told the soldier that none of the family were home—except, that is, for a young boy who had shapeshifted into a werewolf before their terrified eyes. Quite understandably, none of them wanted to hang around to be attacked by the child-beast.

With the petrified group standing on the fringes of the property, the man made his tentative, cautious way toward the house. As he got to the door, the boy loomed into view, although, by now, he had reverted back to his human form. The cavalryman ordered the child to tell him what diabolical activity was afoot in the Feeg house. He soon got an answer, a deeply sinister one.

The boy told the man that his old grandmother—who comes across like a wizened old witch in the story—possessed a magical strap that, when he wore it, would transform him into a wolf. Incredibly, when asked to prove his claims, the boy did exactly that. The man, however, was leaving nothing to chance. He told the boy not to tie the strap around himself until he, the man, was safely in the loft and with the stepladder out of the hands of the child. Now safe from attack, the somewhat skeptical man essentially said, "Do your worst." He did.

As the boy placed the belt around himself, an uncanny transformation occurred, and he, in an astonishingly quick fashion, mutated into the form of a large, formidable wolf. The beast-boy raced out of the front door, terrorizing the group of children, who by now had tentatively gotten closer to the property, to the point where they fled for their lives. The werewolf then raced back into the house, flung off the belt, and immediately transformed back into human form. Despite the boy's savage state when in definitive werewolf mode, while in human form he was placid and even polite—even to the point of letting the cavalry officer examine the belt, which, to him, exhibited no abnormal traits at all.

The man soon made an exit and shared his strange story with a local forester, who nearly immediately concluded the werewolf boy and the elusive, bulletproof wolf that had plagued the landscape for so long were one and the very same. The hunter proved to be highly proactive: he secured a number of silver bullets, vowing to slay the beast, once and for all. As luck would have it, the monster soon put in a return appearance. At first, it was the same old story: regular bullets seemingly had no effect on the creature. Frustration abounded among the hunter's friends. He, however, equipped with silver bullets—the arch-foe of the werewolf—had far more luck, hitting the animal in one of its hind legs. It fell to the ground with a pained howl. It was, however, too powerful for the hunters and suddenly leapt up and bounded away toward the town.

Due to its injury, the werewolf was unable to outrun the hunters, who carefully followed it. It soon became clear that the terrible thing was heading for the Feeg home. As it shot through the door, the group followed. They entered the house, slowly and carefully, but the wolf-thing was nowhere to be seen. At least, not right away. With no sign of the beast in the living room or kitchen, a search of the bedrooms was made. Pay dirt was soon hit. Lying in one of the beds was an old lady, none other than the creepy crone and grandmother to the young boy-monster. To the group's horror, the witch did not appear entirely human: a large, powerful, hair-covered tail hung over the side of the bed. The aged hag, in her state of pain from the piercing bullet, had not fully shapeshifted back into her human form.

What became of the woman and her grandchild is unknown. What we do know, however, is that nineteenth-century werewolf chronicler Karl Bartsch deeply investigated the story, a story that still circulates among the approximately 13,000 people who today call Ludwigslust their home.

Wolf-Headed Humanoids

Scotland's Shetland Islands have more than a few legends of shapeshifters attached to them. Black cats and sea-based "manimals" are two of many. Then there is the Wulver. It is just about the closest thing that Scotland has to a real-life werewolf. It's also a creature that particularly caught the attention of an expert on Scottish legends, a woman by the name of Jessie Margaret Saxby. In her 1932 book, *Shetland Traditional Lore*, she described the Wulver as being a man-sized, and man-shaped, beast that was covered in a coat of brown hair and had a head that was nearly identical to that of a wolf.

Oddly, for the most part—and in stark contrast to the werewolf of the rest of Europe—the Wulver was neither violent nor savage, and, providing that people left it alone, it would do likewise, wrote Saxby. It was most often seen fishing in streams and in the surrounding waters of the islands, sometimes leaving a few fish on the doorsteps of the villagers. That is not to say that the Wulver didn't have its dark side: it most definitely did, as we shall now see.

Jessie Margaret Saxby was not the only person who took a keen interest in the stories of the Wulver. Elliott O'Donnell, an expert on werewolf lore and legend and the author of a 1912 book titled *Werewolves*, also became fascinated by the man-beast of the Shetland Islands. One story that particularly stands out came to O'Donnell from one Andrew Warren, a local. Warren explained to O'Donnell that as a teenager he lived on the islands with his grand-father, who held a senior position in the local church. He was also a keen collector of fossils. On one occasion, the old man discovered in a small, dried-up lake an old human skeleton. This particular skeleton was unlike any other, however: its skull was that of a wolf.

Young Warren and his grandfather carried the skeleton back to their home, specifically leaving it outside. That is when distinctly strange events suddenly erupted. As night fell upon the area, War-ren was left alone, as his grandfather was at the church on business. Suddenly, and while reading a book, he heard a curious scratch-ing noise coming from the kitchen. On entering it, Warren was shocked to see a dark, vague, wolf-like head peering at him through the glass—a head that sat upon what looked like a human neck.

Warren wondered for a few fraught moments if what he was seeing was actually nothing stranger than an optical illusion. It clearly was not. That much became obvious when the vague ap-pearance became fully formed: sharp teeth, an undeniable snarl-like appearance, green eyes, pointed ears, and slim hands with long fingernails were all quickly in evidence. There was no doubt in Warren's mind that the man-monster was utterly evil. Warren made the sign of a cross, but it had absolutely no effect on the ani-mal: it continued to malevolently stare at the frightened boy.

Terrified that the presumed Wulver would eventually try and break in, Warren fled the kitchen and stayed in the hallway, waiting for his grandfather to return. When the old man finally got home and shaken Warren told him of what had taken place, they quickly decided that the best course of action would be to take the skeleton back to where they originally found it and bury it—which is exactly what they did, and immediately, too.

The Wulver—or, more likely, its spirit form—was apparently satisfied by their decision, since it never again bothered Andrew Warren or his grandfather.

The Werewolf of Defiance, Ohio

Located in northwest Ohio, the small and picturesque town of Defiance is home to around 17,000 people and has origins that date back to the latter part of the eighteenth century. In the summer of 1972, Defiance became a hotspot for monster-seekers when locals reported a shapeshifting werewolf in their midst. Thankfully, the beast did not stay around for too long; but from July to August of that year the man-beast most assuredly left its creepy calling card, and, as a result, the town was quickly under siege. Children were kept indoors after school. The local police carefully combed the neighborhood, by day and night. And werewolf fever was just about everywhere in town.

The very first encounter occurred on July 25 in the very early hours of the morning. The unfortunate soul who came face to face with the creature was a railroad employee, working an early-hours shift. As the man switched a train to another track on the Norfolk and Western railroad—in the area of Fifth Street and Swift and Co.—he was suddenly confronted by a large, humanoid figure that had apparently been stalking him from the shadows.

In August 2016, the author visited the site of many of the
Defiance, Ohio, wolfman encounters of 1972.

Dressed in ragged clothing, covered in dark hair, and with a face
that closely resembled that of a wolf or a German Shepherd dog,
it rendered the man frozen to the spot with overwhelming terror.
That was most unfortunate, given that the fanged beast had a large
brick in its huge paw, which it used to pound the fear-filled man
on his left shoulder. Fortunately for the hysterical man, the beast
raced off into the darkness, leaving his shaking victim curled up
into a ball on the floor. And there was something else, too: the
night of the attack was a full moon. That was hardly the end of
things, however. Rather, matters had just begun. Other railroad
employees, including Tom Jones and Ted Davis had notable tales to
tell. According to Davis—cited by journalist James Stegall in an article for the Ohio-based newspaper, *The Blade*, in an August 2, 1972,
article titled, "Werewolf Case in Defiance Not Viewed Lightly by

Police"—"I was connecting an air hose between two cars and was looking down. I saw these huge hairy feet, then I looked up and he was standing there with that big stick over his shoulder. When I started to say something, he took off for the woods."

Jones, also quoted in Stegall's article, was far more concise, describing the beast as "wooly."

The local media was at least partly responsible for the growing controversy. A week later, on August 2, the city's *Crescent News* ran an article titled "Horror Movie Now Playing on Fifth Street," a reference to the location of the initial attack. Then, one day later, on August 3, the newspaper ran a second article, "Wolfman Reports Persist." Its subtitle was suitably spine chilling: "The Shadow of the Wolfman stalked Defiance Again Last Night."

August 3 was also the date on which yet another report was made, this time on Deatrick and South Clinton Street. The single witness, a man, was making his way to the Henry Hotel at around 1:00 a.m. when he developed a deep and unsettling feeling of being followed. Such was his level of terror that after racing to the police station, he spent the rest of the night in the hotel lobby, fearful of what might be waiting for him should he dare to venture outside and into the darkness of the city.

The staff of the *Crescent News* knew a good story when they saw it, hence the August 4 article, "One Wolfman Report Logged." The story was growing by the day. The Toledo-based Ohio newspaper *The Blade* also got in on the act. The title of their article reflected the police's attitude to the matter: "Werewolf Case in Defiance Not Viewed Lightly by Police."

In a city the size of Defiance, it didn't take long at all before just about everyone had heard of the crazed werewolf in their midst. One of those was a woman whose home backed onto the railroads. She was someone very keen to speak to the police when word of the potentially deadly attacks got around. For three nights running, the woman informed the police, she was woken up by the sound of someone violently turning back and forth the knob to her front door. Someone, or *something*, was trying to get in the house. Of course, it could have been a burglar. Except for one thing: on each occasion a low and disturbing growl could be heard directly outside.

Police Chief Don F. Breckler urged calm and told the citizens of Defiance not to try and take on the monster themselves but to dial 911 immediately and let the police handle the situation. He added, "We don't know what to think. We didn't release [the details of the story] when we got the first report about a week ago. But now we're taking it seriously. We're concerned for the safety of our people."

It was also the police who suggested a down-to-earth explanation for the weird affair. Namely, that the creature may have been a burglar wearing a werewolf mask to hide his real identity. Not an impossible scenario, but it's important to note that of those who saw the thing at close quarters, all were unanimous on one point: it was covered in hair from head to toe. Wearing a werewolf mask is not a difficult task. Covering one's entire body with fake hair would be far less easy. No wonder many scoffed at the idea of a masked burglar on the loose. Even the police noted this, admitting that on werewolf or burglar, "there is a lot of natural hair, too." Quite!

When this particular story reached the media, other people came forward, all claiming that the man-monster had tried to force its way into their homes—always in the early hours and sometimes leaving deep and long scratch marks on the front doors, something the police were careful to photograph and add to their quickly growing werewolf file.

As the publicity grew and grew, other railroad workers—also working night shifts—came forward to say that while they had not been attacked by the creature, they had certainly seen it. But, for the most part, they had previously stayed silent for fear of ridicule. By now, however, no one was laughing. At all.

It was as a result of this collective body of data that the police were able to put together a composite picture of the sinister shape-shifter. By all accounts, it stood at a height of around eight feet. The hair on its body was coarse looking and short. And the fact that the creature was clothed led many to believe the inevitable: this was a man who, whether by choice or not, was able to take on the form of a werewolf. Of course, that the clothes—jeans and a shirt but no footwear—were always ragged and torn and the beast was around eight feet in height provoked a theory that in his normal form the man was of regular height and build. But, when the terrifying transformation took place, he grew in size and burst out of his clothes in a style very much befitting Marvel Comics's *The Incredible Hulk*!

Nighttime and early-hours encounters continued well into August, as did sightings of the huge beast in the vicinity of the railroad tracks. And, then, as mid-August arrived, the beast was gone, never to return. Thus ended what was, without doubt, the weirdest, and most fear-filled, saga in the history of Defiance, Ohio.

2
The Horrors of Hexham

NOW, IT'S TIME TO take a look at a mysterious matter involving werewolves invading bedrooms in the dead of night, human sacrifice, and—at the heart of it all—two young boys who may have inadvertently unleashed something ancient and abominable.

Despite its exterior veneer of pleasant old villages, historic castles, and rolling green fields, England is an absolute beacon for monstrous activity. And that includes shapeshifters—and in relatively recent times, too. Our story begins in a northeastern England town called Hexham. Situated in the county of Northumberland, the small town's origins go back to the seventh century. Today, less than 12,000 people call Hexham their home, which is dominated by the centuries-old Hexham Abbey. Back in the early 1970s, however, it was dominated by something else: werewolves.

Not unlike the story played out in *Silver Bullet*—a 1985 movie of wolfman-proportions based on Stephen King's *Cycle of the Werewolf* and starring Gary Busey, Megan Follows, and Corey Haim—the story revolves around a pair of youngsters who find themselves up to their necks in monstrous matters. Although, by the time the whole thing was over, they surely wished they had stayed away from it. Let's take a trip back to February 1972 and the home of

Colin Robson and his brother, Leslie, two young, preteen boys who were about to unearth something … well … unearthly! And I *do* mean that literally.

In his book *Quest for the Hexham Heads*, Paul Screeton tells of how, as young and adventurous boys are wont to do, the brothers spent one particular morning playing and digging in the backyard of the family home. As they did so, they uncovered not too far below the surface of the yard a pair of strange-looking heads; they were made out of stone, about the size of a baseball, and had been carved in a decidedly primitive fashion. Nevertheless, it was pretty clear that one was intended to represent a female and the other a male. Both looked slightly ominous—creepy even. But for young Colin and Leslie, they were downright exciting. The boys played with them for a while and then took them into the house. And what a mistake that proved to be.

No sooner had the weird heads been taken into the house than all hell broke loose. Some might say, after reading this, that the hell parallels are all too appropriate. Placed on a shelf, the heads were seen to shuffle along, slowly yet creepily, of course. Ornaments in the house inexplicably shattered. And Colin and Leslie's sister suffered an explosion of glass from a window as she slept. It was a collective and ominous state of affairs that soon spilled over into the house next door. A few strange events were about to be replaced by absolute monster mayhem.

Barely forty-eight hours after the heads of Hexham were dug up and taken into the Robson home, the Dodd family suffered a series of what can only be described as paranormal assaults. It was late at night when Ellen Dodd and her daughter had a frightening encounter with a beast that materialized in their home. It was a bipedal monster with the head of a wolf. For a second or two, it stared malevolently at both mother and daughter and then raced out of the room. The unmistaken sound of something large and heavy running down the staircase immediately followed, as did the sound of the front door being opened. The werewolf-like thing had come and gone in an instant. It wasn't long before word got around that the diabolical heads had somehow provoked—or invoked—the man-monster to manifest. And it wasn't long before the Robson family wanted the heads gone.

It turns out that those sinister heads reached the eager hands of Dr. Anne Ross, as Paul Screeton reveals in *Tales of the Hexham Heads*; she was an expert in the field of Celtic history and strongly suspected the heads uncovered by the boys were Celtic in origin. Not only that, Dr. Ross had written a number of relevant books, including *Pagan Celtic Britain*, and was someone who had seen very similarly fashioned old heads on various previous occasions. Incredibly, she suspected they were created around 2,000 years ago and may have been used in fertility or sacrificial rites to ancient earth gods or both. Maybe even more than that. It was when she took the Hexham heads into her Southampton home—which was close to 150 miles from where the Robson family lived—that the crazed activity began again. On one particular night, she was suddenly woken from her sleep by the presence of a hideous monster looming over the bed in menacing fashion.

Dr. Ross described the manimal as being roughly two meters in height with a stooped stance and completely black in color. Practically frozen in the bed, she saw the beast long enough to see that the upper portion of its body was all wolf, whereas the lower part of its torso and its legs were definitively human-like, albeit covered in hair or fur. As was the case at the Robson home, the man-thing suddenly leapt out of the bedroom. And so did Dr. Ross: she jumped out of the bed and raced out of the room. She heard its heavy padding, which placed it somewhere toward the rear of her property by now. It was soon gone, engulfed by the darkness of the early hours.

Then, not long afterward, Dr. Ross's daughter, Berenice, caught sight of the monster, too—she also described it as something half human and half wolf. Then, in no time, the entire family developed a sense of profound unease and malevolence in the house—almost as if it had somehow been supernaturally infected or paranormally polluted. As for the heads, well, they just had to go. Dr. Ross was done with them.

Hardly surprisingly, among the archaeological community—and also within the paranormal research community of that time— the Hexham heads very quickly became as notorious as they were feared. They were soon handed over to an expert on ancient mysteries, Don Robins. But not for long. Then they landed on the doorstep of an expert in the field of dowsing—also known as water divining— named Frank Hyde. Having dowsed the heads very carefully, Hyde was deeply troubled by what he found: namely, a sense of menace that seemed to surround him whenever he got too close to the horrific heads. They changed hands again, and again, and … again. Today, their exact location is a matter of great debate within the field of supernatural anomalies. Some say they were destroyed. Others claim to have them in their possession—although widespread suspicions exist that, if anything, they are nothing more than carbon copies of the originals made in very recent times. The mystery remains appropriately that: a mystery.

Beyond the Hexham Heads

There is a very weird afterword to the affair of Hexham's weird, carved heads. When those in the paranormal research community began to look into the mysterious matter, several people decided to take a look into the local library's newspaper archives—chiefly to determine if anything of a similar, sinister nature had ever occurred in and around town. Incredibly, it had. Way back in 1904, specifically on December 10, the local newspaper, the *Hexham Courant*, reported on a strange and potentially dangerous development in and around Hexham. Newspaper staff came straight to the point with their eye-catching headline, "Wolf at Large in Allendale," a reference to a nearby, small village that was experiencing a series of mutilations and deaths of farm animals.

It is important to note why, specifically, this story attracted so much attention: the wolf is extinct in the United Kingdom and has been for several centuries. In other words, not only was it worrying that a wolf—and a very large one, too—was on the loose, it was also deeply baffling. Where did it come from? Why was it targeting the Hexham region? Local villagers and farmers wanted answers. For a while, there were none. All there was, was complete and utter carnage: the first attack resulted in one sheep having its stomach torn open and its entrails ripped, wrenched and dangling from the body of the poor animal. Another sheep was so savagely attacked that all that remained was its skull—which had been chewed clean of meat—and its horns.

It's safe to say that widespread fear gripped both Hexham and Allendale and to a huge degree. In scenes that predated—but eerily paralleled—those old 1930s and '40s Universal Studios monster movies starring the likes of Bela Lugosi and Boris Karloff, the local folk took to the streets, to the hills, and to the surrounding woods, armed with flaming torches, as they sought to find and kill the deadly thing that was now roaming and rampaging among them.

The *Hexham Courant*, in its "Wolf at Large in Allendale" article, continued that children had been told to stay clear of the moors and the woods and to keep to the roads and the busy pathways. The local police were doubling up their presence in the area. And what was termed the Hexham Wolf Committee was hastily created to deal with the monstrous menace. Rather oddly, a team of hunting dogs was brought in from a nearby town and despite their skills, they were unable to catch even a smidgen of the mysterious wolf's scent. It remained wholly, and frustratingly, elusive.

That is, however, until the body of a wolf was found on January 7, 1905, on railroad tracks at the village of Cumwhinton, Cumbria, as Stuart Ferol noted in his 2005 article for *Fortean Times* magazine, "The Hexham Wolf." There were, however, problems with the theory that this particular wolf was the culprit. Of course, the fact that a wolf was found strongly suggested that it was the culprit. But, more than a few people had doubts that it could have carried out such ferocious attacks and without ever leaving any kind of scent whatsoever. The matter was hailed as an end to the tumultuous time, but for more than a few months the people of Hexham and Allendale remained distinctly uneasy—and particularly so late at night.

And still the story is not over. Persistent digging revealed that way back in 1810 the people of Ennerdale, a village in the very same area, became gripped with fear when, across a six-month period, close to 400 sheep were savaged and killed by a mysterious beast that—just like its 1904 counterpart—remained elusive in the extreme. When one of the sheep was found to have been drained of blood, the hysteria levels practically went through the roof. It was this case, along with several other, similar ones, that led to the suspicion that the wolf-like monster had paranormal, rather than physical, origins. Ingenious attempts to kill the beast by placing dead sheep laced with poison on the hills at night completely failed: the creature was way too cunning to fall for that ruse.

On a couple of occasions the animal was seen by handfuls of local folk; they were all sure that what they had seen was an animal that seemed to be part cat and part dog that had noticeable stripes running down its body. This has given rise to the intriguing and amazing theory that the creature might have been a thylacine, a large Tasmanian marsupial that is said to have become extinct in the 1930s but is still occasionally reported in Tasmania to this very day. How such an animal might have found its way to Hexham and Ennerdale is anyone's guess.

In this case, however, there was a solution: the animal was finally shot and killed by a man named John Steel as it sought to escape along the River Ehen. Incredibly, when it was examined, the mysterious and still-unidentified beast was found to weigh—in modern terms—a hefty 51 kilograms (112 pounds). No one was sure of its identity, and although it apparently went on public display for a while, its remains were finally tossed out with the garbage.

Regardless of what the beasts of 1810 and 1904 really were—wolves, supernatural monsters, thylacines, or something else entirely—it's decidedly intriguing that they should have surfaced in the very same area where years later, in 1972, paranormal man-beasts of a werewolf-like nature and appearance were manifesting, specifically in the wake of the discovery of the Hexham heads.

Should the Hexham heads ever circulate again, we may once more see rampaging man-wolves in our midst.

3
SHAPESHIFTING AT THE CEMETERY

THE WOODS AND FORESTS of England are inviting and picturesque. They are, however, filled with terrible things that provoke fear and hysteria. One of them—a hideous shapeshifter—plunged a small community into a collective state of fear in 2007.

The Cannock Chase is a large and ancient area of forest in central England. In 1958, it was officially designated as an "area of outstanding beauty" by the local government. While 1958 is not that long ago at all, it's important to note that the area itself has been a wild and mysterious one not just for decades or even centuries, but for millennia, even. For example, in the village of Cannock Wood, on the fringes of the Chase, stand the remains of an Iron Age hill-fort, one that was constructed by the Cornovii people, a Celtic band that held sway over much of the area at the time. It is known locally as the Castle Ring. Numerous reports of creatures resembling Bigfoot, large black cats, and even a Mothman-like entity with fiery eyes have surfaced from the Castle Ring.

Also demonstrating the historical nature of the Cannock Chase is the "Glacial Boulder," a large chunk of rock that sits in a wild area near the old village of Brocton. That very same chunk of rock, at the height of the last Ice Age, was carried by the movements of the great glaciers from Cniffel, Scotland, to the Chase—a distance of around 170 miles. Add old, labyrinthine, underground mineshafts that pepper the area, as well as a series of notorious murders that occurred between 1965 and 1967, and what you have is a place filled with history and notoriety. The Cannock Chase is most assuredly a place filled with mayhem and mystery.

In 1903, there was a spate of violent horse mutilations in the area that, depending on one's own perspective, were the work of a local man named George Edalji, a pack of trained wild boars, a huge and unknown kind of bird, or even a "hypnotized ape." In more recent years, the Chase has become infamous for its extensive body of supernatural activity. People have reported encounters with Bigfoot-style beasts, with large black cats the size of mountain lions, flying humanoids that bring to mind the United States' Mothman, unidentified and large creatures swimming in the waters of the many deep pools that can be found on the Chase, and a nearly endless supply of UFO encounters, including an alleged Roswell-style UFO crash in early 1964. And then there is the matter of the Cannock Chase's shapeshifters.

The story dates back to 2007 and, somewhat appropriately, to the heart of a certain cemetery on the Chase. Within the Chase is a picturesque area called Broadhurst Green. It's filled with huge, dense trees, numerous streams and ponds, and also what is known as the Cannock Chase German Military Cemetery. It is a large cemetery that houses the remains of almost 5,000 German soldiers and airmen. During both the First and Second World Wars, numerous German military personnel were captured and transferred to prisoner of war camps across the United Kingdom. Many of those same military personnel died during the hostilities and were buried in cemeteries and graveyards closest to where they were previously imprisoned. In 1959, however, the governments of the United Kingdom and Germany reached an agreement that resulted in the remains of the 4,929 Germans who died on British soil all being transferred to one specific location: the then newly constructed Cannock Chase German Military Cemetery. Today, the cemetery is regularly visited by war historians, the families of those Germans who lost their lives, and the public, too. In 2007, however, the cemetery had a new and very different visitor. It was a visitor of nightmarish proportions.

The saga began in March 2007, when a local paranormal investigations group, the West Midlands Ghost Club, found itself on the receiving end of something extremely weird and surely unanticipated: a stash of reports of werewolf-like beasts seen lurking among the old gravestones. The story of how the WMGC came to be involved, and the nature of the encounters can be found at their online article, "But I'm Alright Naaoooooowwwwwww!!!!!"

Such was the interest the reports provoked that Mike Lockley, the then-editor of the local and now defunct newspaper, the *Chase Post*, gave the story a great deal of page space—to the extent that the publicity brought in even more reports. For around three months, the good folk of the Cannock Chase found themselves plunged into a controversy that had at its heart sinister shapeshifting monsters that dwelled among the long dead. It was a controversy that very soon was destined to become filled with terror and hysteria.

The morphing monsters of the Cannock Chase were not typical of the old legends, however. In other words, this was most assuredly not a case of witnesses reporting people changing into werewolves (or vice versa). No, they werewolf-like creatures that had the ability to alter their body structure, thus allowing them to walk both on four legs and on two.

The werewolf-haunted cemetery on England's Cannock Chase.

One of the earliest reports—referenced in the *Stafford Post* newspaper on April 26, 2007, in an article titled "Werewolf Spotted in Stafford"—came from a local postman who, while riding his motorbike past the cemetery on one particular, sunny morning, caught sight of what at first he thought was a large dog walking around the cemetery. It was not a dog at all: it was a walking nightmare. The man was amazed, and more than a little concerned, by what he could soon see was a wolf. But it was a wolf of extraordinary size. That wild wolves have reportedly been extinct in the United Kingdom since 1680 made matters even more amazing. That was the year in which one Sir Ewen Cameron killed a wild wolf in Perthshire, Scotland, quite possibly the very last wild wolf in the entire United Kingdom. Granted, there have been sporadic reports of wolves still inhabiting some of the less travelled, and even less inhabited, parts of the country. Nothing, however, has even surfaced conclusively to demonstrate that wolves have lived in the wilds of the United Kingdom since the seventeenth century. But try telling that to the beasts of a certain cemetery. And good luck telling that to the witnesses, too.

As the man slowed his bike down to a complete stop, he stared in awe and fear as the bulky animal prowled around the gravestones, making it abundantly clear to the man that this was no husky dog or something similar. The stone-cold facts hit the man suddenly and hard: there was a wolf on the Cannock Chase. As the witness watched, entranced and with his heart practically pounding out of his chest, something terrifying and unearthly happened. The wolf caught sight of the man, froze, and stared intently in his direction; its eyes firmly locked on him for a few terrifying seconds. It was then that the body of the four-legged animal began to change, to mutate. The postman could only sit and watch—nearly paralyzed in the spot—as the hind legs of the wolf started to grow in length. Oddly, and for a second or several, the creature became blurry to the eye as its form began to change. Then, with its legs now very much resembling those of a human in shape, the beast reared up on its morphed limbs and took on a bipedal stance. Not surprisingly, all that the man could think of was "werewolf." Fortunately for the witness, the creature raced into the heart of the woods and, within seconds, was gone. It was soon destined to return, however.

Only weeks later, there was yet another encounter in the cemetery. This time the witness was the leader of a local Scouts group. He, too, had the distinct misfortune to cross paths with the monster. And, as was also the case with the postman's experience, the witness at first assumed that what he was seeing was a wolf—perhaps one that had escaped from a private zoo, he initially thought. That theory went completely out the window when the animal shapeshifted into a hairy, humanoid form, rose up onto its back legs—to a height of around seven feet—and charged off into the darkened depths of the surrounding trees.

In a third case, a woman from the nearby town of Rugeley described seeing such a monster barely a two-minute drive from the cemetery late one night in July 2007. On this occasion, the creature was in its upright werewolf form and stood near the edge of a small, tree-shrouded lane as she approached it. She brought her car to a complete halt and, gripping the steering wheel, watched as the creature was enveloped in a blue haze, took on that blurry appearance described by the postman just a couple of months earlier, altered its body shape, and dropped down onto all fours. In seconds it was gone. And so was the woman, who quickly drove home in a state of ice-cold terror.

Altogether, thirteen such reports surfaced between early March and late August 2007—and, it should be noted, who knows how many more went unreported—after which the sightings abruptly and oddly stopped. It is intriguing to note, however, that several local residents, spurred on by the coverage given by the *Chase Post*, reported that they had encountered another unusual creature at the cemetery. Namely, a large black cat, one that was roughly the size of a German Shepherd dog and possibly even a bit bigger. Incredibly, a story also surfaced of a hair-covered humanoid, barely three feet tall, seen in 1959 and in and around the very same area where the cemetery now stands. These additional encounters, with other odd and out-of-place animals, led to notable speculation that the wolf, the werewolf, the hairy dwarf, and the black cat were all one and the same—a monster that lurked in the cemetery and that had the ability to take on the form of just about any and every creature that crossed its beastly mind.

A Werewolf and the Military

Also in 2007, and in response to an article I wrote at my blog *There's Something in the Woods* ("Do Werewolves Roam the Woods of England?") a man named Wes posted a comment to the blog, detailing his very own sighting of an upright wolf-like animal, thirty-seven years earlier. Wes said,

> I encountered a werewolf (lack of better description) in England in 1970, I was 20 yrs. old when I was stationed at RAF Alconbury [a British Royal Air Force base situated in Huntingdon, England]. I was in a secure weapons storage area when I encountered it. It seemed shocked and surprised to [have] been caught off guard and I froze in total fright. I was armed with a .38 and never once considered using it. There was no aggression on its part. I could not comprehend what I was seeing. It is not human. It has a flat snout and large eyes. Its height is approx 5 ft and weight approx. 200 lbs. It is very muscular and thin. It wore no clothing and was only moderately hairy. It ran away on its hind legs and scurried over a chain link fence and ran deep into the dense wooded area adjacent to the base. I was extremely frightened but the fear developed into a total commitment of trying to contact it again. I was obsessed with it. I was able to see it again a few weeks later at a distance in the wooded area. I watched it for about 30 seconds slowly moving through the woods and I will never forget my good fortune to encounter it … and to know this "creature" truly does lives among us.

Interestingly, and as is the case with so many locations where shapeshifters are seen, RAF Alconbury has been the site of more than one supernatural mystery. For example, on the night of September 14, 1994, a large, black, triangular-shaped UFO was seen both flying by and hovering over the base by several amazed drivers—a story told to me by one of the witnesses several years later. Equally intriguing, in the winter of 1999, a large and fiery-eyed black dog was encountered by a guard at the base who personally shared his story with me in 1999, albeit with an assurance of anonymity. It was around 3:00 a.m. when the huge hound was seen walking near a brightly illuminated weapons storage area. The guard in question, who was around seventy or eighty feet away from the dog, called it over—assuming, at the time, that it was perhaps lost and had managed to wander onto the base. At the sound of the man's words, the dog stopped in its tracks, turned, and walked toward him—which proved not to be a good thing.

It was at that point, with the dog's face in the guard's line of view, that the glowing red eyes of the beast could be seen. The guard, unsure what to do, simply stood there and did absolutely nothing. Aside, that is, from staring, mouth agape, as the approximately four-foot-tall animal walked past him with a malevolent look on its face. It growled loudly and deeply as it did so. Shock immediately set in for the guard when the huge hound vanished before his eyes. Perhaps wisely, he chose not to file an incident report. And who can blame him?

As we will see later—and particularly so in relation to a 2007 encounter of a man named Martin Whitley with a huge black dog on Dartmoor in England—body-morphing and black dogs go together in hand-in-glove style. This provokes an intriguing question: was Wes's werewolf seen at RAF Alconbury in 1970 the very same beast that was encountered at the base twenty-nine years later, albeit in phantom hound form? That both beasts have a long history of shapeshifting makes such a possibility not at all implausible.

4
BRIDGE BEASTS

ALL ACROSS THE WORLD, one can find tales of strange creatures that lurk on, around, and below ancient bridges. More than a few of those tales revolve around the world of the shapeshifter. They appear to have a particular liking for bridges—something that is worth keeping in mind, should you find yourself crossing an old bridge late one night when the moon is full.

Her name might be inclined to provoke laughter and amusement in some quarters, but there is nothing to joke about when it comes to the matter of the Donkey Woman of San Antonio, Texas. She is a terrifying shapeshifter who haunts a particular old bridge in a suburb of San Antonio known as Elm Creek. Her strange story is one that began in the latter part of the nineteenth century. So the old tale goes, the woman in question resided with her family in a run-down wooden shack on the edge of the creek in question. They earned their living from rearing chickens, pigs, and goats and selling them to the local folk. Life was hard, but the woman, her husband, and her two children—a boy and a girl—got by and, by all accounts, had a happy life. That is, until one day, when a certain man arrived on the scene and tragedy and death soon followed in his ominous wake.

Although the family did not know the man, they were fully aware of his reputation—which was that of a cruel, spoilt local tyrant. In his early twenties, the man didn't need to work: his father was a powerful figure in a nearby community and someone with a large house, acres upon acres of land, and a great deal of money, much of which went to the son. He was a disturbing character, someone who got his kicks from hurting, and even killing, animals. When the man happened to be riding near the family home one particular morning, he caught sight of their pet mule, doing nothing but happily munching on the grass of the small field that the family owned.

The man brought his horse to a standstill, jumped off it, and began punching the mule—both in its face and on its body. When the mule understandably began to cry out, both husband and wife ran to the field to see what on earth was going down, their first thought being that perhaps the mule was being attacked by the likes of a mountain lion or something similar. When, however, they saw the young man assaulting their mule, they quickly retaliated with a barrage of rocks, several of which caught the man on the arms and back. He immediately turned his attention away from the mule and vowed that they would pay for their actions—actions, ironically, that his crazed character had provoked in the first place. And pay they did, unfortunately.

In the early hours of the following morning, and as the landscape was blanketed by darkness, a group of men hired by that aforementioned spoilt tyrant stealthily descended on the family home. They torched it as the family slept. Such was the speed with which the old, wooden building burned that the two children were unfortunately burnt to death. As for their father, he received a bullet to the brain, which killed him instantly. The woman, meanwhile, was fried to a crisp and managed to stagger her way to Elm

Creek, into which she plunged, never to be seen again. At least, not in human form.

In the immediate years that followed, reports regularly surfaced of sightings of a frightening-looking woman with the head of what appeared to be a donkey. She would prowl around the area where her dead family lived and her destroyed home once stood. That the skin of the strange woman was described as blackened, burnt and smoldering is a solid indication that this was the spectral form of the murdered woman. There was, however, another aspect to this saga—one that revolves around the matter of shapeshifting.

A local rumor—one that, to this very day, still persists in the Elm Creek area of San Antonio—suggests that the Donkey Woman returned from the grave as not part-woman and part-donkey after all but as a combination of human and mule. So the story goes, the spirit form of the woman, angered by what was done to not just her family, but also to their pet mule, returned to our plain of existence in the form of what might most accurately be termed a mule-woman. She has most often been seen at what is called Elm Creek Bridge. Could it be the case that after death we can come back and shapeshift into the form of something that is half animal and half human? That is precisely the theory that circulates among those who live in the Elm Creek area and who take the legend of the animal woman very seriously. Even in the twenty-first century, shapeshifting in South Texas is perceived as being all too real. Perhaps the people of the area know something the rest of us do not.

The Revenant of the Bridge

It is a dark, cold, and wind-swept night in early 1879. The location: the fringes of a centuries-old little village in central England. A man is crossing a large stone bridge that spans an ancient canal. His only company on that night is a faithful horse, which is dutifully pulling behind it a battered, aged wooden cart. After a busy day spent moving furniture, the man is tired, hungry and thirsty. He decides to make a welcome stop at the village's pleasant inn, for a pint or two of beer and a hot meal. Unfortunately, before he can do so, fate intervenes. And it does so in just about the most traumatic and horrific way possible.

The man is barely halfway across the bridge when, suddenly, out of the thick bushes and trees that surround the bridge and dominate the canal, a large, chimpanzee-like beast—sporting wild, glowing eyes—leaps out of the darkness and charges in his direction. For a moment, he is paralyzed on the spot, gripped by overwhelming, cold fear. At the very last moment, however, the infernal monster swerves to one side and makes a mighty leap aboard the cart, terrifying the poor horse in the process.

Bridge 39, the lair of the Man-Monkey.

The crazed, shaggy man-monster stands tall and imposing, its legs spread wide and its arms waving toward the heavens in wild fashion. The man quickly gathers his wits, grabs the horse's whip, and proceeds to beat the beast to a pulp. At least, that is what he tries to do. To his eternal terror, the whip passes right through the body of the ape-like thing that is raging before him. In his state of near-hysteria the man can only conclude that he missed the animal, so he strikes it again. Once more, the whip has absolutely no effect—other than to demonstrate that the monster is one of spectral, rather than flesh-and-blood, proportions. Before he can decide what to do next, the monster leaps off the cart and races toward an old, dusty path that leads down to the shadowy canal below. In seconds, it is out of sight.

The man takes a deep breath, calms down his fraught horse and carefully scans the area. Thankfully, the monster does not return. At least, not tonight it doesn't. He has just had an encounter with a highly dangerous monster that is destined to quickly become known as the Man-Monkey. It's time to calm those fraught nerves and to share the traumatic experience with a few friends over a couple of flagons of old English ale.

The story I have just told is not one of fiction. Far from it, in fact: it is all too terrifyingly real. The date was January 21, 1879. The location was Bridge 39, which spans the centuries-old Shropshire Union Canal. The village was Ranton, situated in the English county of Staffordshire, an ancient hamlet which dates back approximately 1,000 years. And the pub in which the scared-witless soul told his story to an audience of frightened locals was the seventeenth century–era Hand and Cleaver. Since that fateful night, more than two dozen reports have been made of this strange and sinister creature—which can best be described as something akin to a spectral, ghostly Bigfoot. It may, however, be something even stranger than that. In a very strange and disturbing way, it just might be a shapeshifter of a very dark and deadly variety.

The first person to ever investigate the saga of the Man-Monkey was a nineteenth-century writer named Charlotte Burne. She was a woman with a deep passion for and an extensive knowledge of Staffordshire history and legend. She quickly paid Ranton a visit. In doing so, she soon gained the confidence of the people of the village and even spoke with the local police about the macabre mystery. It was the latter conversation that led to something notable. The village's solitary police constable confided in Burne that sightings of the Man-Monkey had begun just three weeks earlier. Not only that, the encounters kicked off just two days after a local man drowned in the canal—and only around fifty feet from where the large bridge continues to stand to this very day, barely a stone's throw from the darkness where the Man-Monkey first emerged.

According to the police constable, the belief in Ranton—which was generally discussed in distinctly hushed tones—was that the Man-Monkey was the drowned man returned from the dead, shape-shifted into the form of a terrible, hair-covered beast. Eye-opening is the fact that Charlotte Burne had come across very similar tales from other parts of Staffordshire. She said in her 1883 book, *Shropshire Folk-Lore*, that the overriding theory locally was that the Man-Monkey represented "a human revenant," one who haunted Bridge 39 "in animal form." Its physical appearance, that of "a strange black creature with great white eyes," added Burne, "resonates with contemporary accounts of ghostly activity elsewhere."

In my 2007 book, *Man-Monkey*, Dr. David Clarke, a folklorist who has also addressed cases similar to that of the Man-Monkey, states that at least as far back as 600 years ago there was a widespread belief in certain parts of England that those who died in violent fashion—whether the victims of murder or the victims of suicide—returned to our plane of existence in the morphed forms of malignant and marauding beasts. They were destined to exist in a nightmarish state of purgatory—the direct result of their unforgivable actions, as the people of that era saw things, at least. This was an issue that also greatly interested Elliott O'Donnell, a man who penned numerous books on paranormal phenomena, including a still widely acclaimed 1912 book on the world's most famous shapeshifters, *Werewolves*.

O'Donnell said, in the pages of *Werewolves*, something that closely echoed the words of Charlotte Burne: "It is an old belief that the souls of cataleptic and epileptic people, during the body's unconsciousness, adjourned temporarily to animals, and it is therefore only in keeping with such a view to suggest that on the deaths of such people their spirits take permanently the form of animals. This would account for the fact that places where cataleptics and idiots have died are often haunted by semi and by wholly animal types of phantasms."

Should you ever find yourself, late one night, in the vicinity of the Shropshire Union Canal's Bridge 39, take very careful heed of all the above. A deadly, form-changing monster may be just mere meters away, hiding amid the trees and ready to launch an all-out attack, just as it did way back in January 1879. And just as it may well continue to do so for all of eternity.

Old Stinker on the Loose

In April 2016, a very strange story surfaced out of the north of England. Not just the local media but the national media, too, were busy chasing down the strange and sinister story of what has become known as the Werewolf of Hull, reportedly an eight-foot-tall, hair-covered monster. The case was, however, notable for the fact that several of the witnesses claimed the beast shapeshifted from a terrible, foul monster into the form of a black-cloaked old witch.

Most of the reports surfaced in and around the vicinity of what is called the Beverley and Barmston Drain, a land drainage operation, the origins of which date back to the latter part of the 1800s. A tunnel that carries the drain can be found below an old bridge on Beverley Beck, a canal in East Riding, Yorkshire, England—a location where a number of the encounters with the hair-covered thing have taken place. The bridge connection is an important one that should not be overlooked.

In her 2006 book, *Mystery Big Cats*, author Merrily Harpur provides the following words on what she terms "liminal zones": "These are the transitional zones between one area and another— the kind of no-man's-land traditionally regarded as magical." Harpur's research has shown that such zones include streams, gates, churchyards, and bridges. With that in mind, there's a good chance something of a definitively supernatural nature is afoot at the Beverley and Barmston Drain.

In December 2015, a woman said to me, "It stood upright one moment. The next it was down on all fours running like a dog. I was terrified." Of course, this is very similar to the reports coming out of the Cannock Chase in 2007 of a dog-/wolf-like creature that had the ability to run on both two legs and four—a case which has already been dissected.

Even more controversial was the story of a husband and wife who claimed to have seen the monster of the Beverley Beck canal feast on a dead dog and then bound over a fence more than two meters in height—and with the remains of the poor dog clamped in its jaws. Very wisely, the couple's very own dog made it abundantly clear it had no wish to head down to the canal. It may be no coincidence that as the fear-filled couple—and their equally terrified pet—fled the scene, they briefly saw a black-cloaked old woman cackling at them from the edge of the canal.

Even the local authorities had gotten involved. Labor councilor Steve Wilson was quoted by Jen Mills at *Metro* as saying, "I am happy to keep a diary of sightings by people around here and report them to Hull council." Although, what the local council might be able to do about a rampaging werewolf on the loose is anyone's guess. Arm the local police with silver bullets, perhaps?

So, what might the creature be? The United Kingdom's media picked up—and picked up quickly and widely—on a local legend of an abominable beast known as "Old Stinker." It's a terrifying half-human, half-animal thing that has a long history in the area—one that dates back centuries. So the story goes, its name is taken from the legend that it allegedly suffered from severely bad breath! And its physical appearance was said to have been no better either: it was covered in hair and had piercing and glowing red eyes. On top of that, it regularly devoured the corpses of the recent dead. As for the hunting grounds of Old Stinker, they were said to be the Yorkshire Wolds, which—interestingly—are just north of the Beverley and Barmston Drain. Most relevant of all, Old Stinker could morph into numerous forms, including a wolf, a bear, and a large black cat—which eerily parallels the saga of a body-changing beast seen and photographed on Dartmoor in England in 2007 by a man named Martin Whitley—a case we will come to in due course.

Have we seen the recent and sudden resurrection of a very old monster that can transform itself from beast to beast and even to human? Maybe so.

5
SHAPE-CHANGERS
OF THE WATER

MOVING ON FROM SHAPESHIFTERS of woods, cemeteries, and bridges, now is the time to address the matter of yet another breed of morphing monster. This one lurks in the lakes and rivers of our world.

For centuries, Scottish folklore and legend have both been filled with tales of a wild and deadly beast known as the kelpie. The terrible beast, which has the ability to transform itself into numerous forms—even that of people—was greatly feared throughout the 1600s and 1700s, when reports of the kelpie were at their height. As for its curious name, "kelpie" is a term meaning "water-horse." There is a very good reason as to why that particular name was applied to the beast, as will soon become very clear. As its name strongly suggests, the water-horse spent much of its time lurking in the waters of Scottish lochs—specifically in the shallower, marshy areas of such locales. It would coldly and callously wait for an unwary passerby to appear on the scene and then strike, mercilessly and without any hint of a warning. The beast's mode of attack was, admittedly, ingenious, even if the end result for the victim was not a good one. In fact, it was almost always downright fatal.

Very much creatures of the night, kelpies were said to dwell in the waters of literally dozens of Scottish lochs. As creature-seeker Roland Watson demonstrated in his book *The Water Horses of Loch Ness*, however, the vast majority of reports of such beasts emanate from none other than Loch Ness, the home of what is arguably the world's most famous lake monster, Nessie—which we shall address shortly.

We may never know for sure the real form of the kelpie—only the guise that led to the creation of its name. But what we can say for certain is that the small number of witnesses who encountered the beast, and who lived to tell the tale, described it as a large black or white horse. In most cases, the victim was a late-night traveler, walking along an old, well-known pathway near the water's edge of the relevant loch. Suddenly, the huge horse would rise out of the water, dripping wet, and make its way to the shore, with its coat shining under the light of the moon.

Under such strange circumstances, many might be inclined to make a run for it immediately. There is, however, a very strange aspect to many of the kelpie stories. Namely, that the people who crossed its path felt as if their free will had been taken from them and that they were deliberately prevented from fleeing the scene. Today, we might justifiably suggest that the beast had the power to control the minds of those in its deadly sights, perhaps even by a form of supernatural hypnosis. Those fortunate enough to escape the icy clutches of the kelpie described how they felt driven to climb on the back of the horse and grab its reins. Despite having a sense of dread and a fear of doing so, that's exactly what so many did—and, in the process, they failed to survive and tell their tale. It was at that point that the kelpie made its move—an incredibly fast move.

With the entranced person now atop the monster, it would suddenly launch itself into the deep and cold waters of the loch, with the poor soul unable to let go of the reins. Death by drowning was all but inevitable, aside from that very lucky aforementioned body of people who were fortunate enough to have survived and relate their stories—hence why we know of the creature and its terrible modus operandi. As for the reason behind these deadly attacks, it was said that the creatures sought one thing more than any other: the human soul.

When word of the murderous monster got out among the people of the small hamlets and villages of ancient Scotland, the kelpie cunningly chose to take on another form, given that its cover—as a large horse—had now been blown, of course. That form was a beautiful woman with long hair dressed in a flowing robe. Her (or, rather, *its*) targets were always men, and again walking home late at night, perhaps after a few pints of beer at a local inn or after toiling in the fields until dark. The she-devil would, just like its horse-based form, beckon the entranced man to the water's edge. She would then take his hand and slowly lead him into the loch, careful step by careful step. Then, when the man was around waist deep, she would violently drag him below the water, drowning him in seconds and mercilessly stealing his soul.

Legend also tells of the kelpie taking on the form of a large, hairy, ape-like animal. Notably, Scotland has a long history of Bigfoot-type creatures in its midst—which may not be a coincidence, given what we know of the kelpie, its shapeshifting skills, and its Scottish origins. All of these bring us back to the dark heart of Loch Ness.

As I noted earlier, Nessie authority Roland Watson has determined that the vast majority of centuries-old sightings and reports of kelpies emanated from Loch Ness. This, obviously, provokes an important question: could the Nessies of today and the kelpies of yesteryear be one and the very same thing? It's a highly valid question, since it would seem most unlikely for the loch to be populated by two different kinds of unknown animals. As for the answer, it is almost certainly the case that far from being the flesh and blood beasts that so many assume the Nessies to be, the creatures are indeed kelpies, but in far more modern—and very different—incarnations.

The image that any mention of the Loch Ness Monster provokes is almost always that of a long-necked, hump-backed animal with four flippers and a powerful tail. Certainly, that's how the media and movie-makers portray the Nessies and even how numerous witnesses have described them. Such descriptions provoke images of long-extinct marine reptiles known as plesiosaurs—animals that became extinct around sixty-five million years ago. It is a little-known fact, however, that the unknown animals of Loch Ness come in all shapes and sizes, something that adds even more weight to the theories that they are shapeshifting kelpies and not merely unknown animals or surviving relics from times long past.

Contrary to the popular assumption that the Nessies closely resemble plesiosaurs, more than a few eyewitnesses to the monsters have described them in an astonishing variety of different ways. Such as (take a deep breath) giant-sized frogs; tusked, camel-like, or crocodile-type entities; beasts that completely lack the long neck that so many people have reported; animals closely resembling salamanders; and creatures with feet, rather than the so-often reported flippers. In many of the cases, such descriptions were made by people who were able to see the monsters at very close quarters—strongly suggesting they were not mistaken about what it was they encountered.

It is beyond absurd to try and assert that Loch Ness might harbor six or seven different types of amazing animals, never mind just one! There is only one reasonable conclusion available to us: the Nessies of today and the kelpies of the past are one and the same.

Constantly shifting their shapes as they see fit is the name of their ominous game. Their motivation: the stealing of the human soul.

An Ape-Man Becomes a River Monster

In the summer of 1976, yet another encounter with the much-feared Man-Monkey occurred at Bridge 39 on the Shropshire Union Canal. The witness was a man named Paul, a keen fisherman and someone who in July and August 1976 spent several Saturdays out at the canal with his rods, reels, bait, cans of beer, and his favorite beef and onion sandwiches, soaking in the intense heat. Paul told me that on one particular Saturday afternoon, he was sitting near the water's edge on a small wooden stool that he always carried with him when he was "literally frozen solid" by the sight of "what at first I thought was a big log floating down the cut, about sixty or seventy feet away." According to Paul, however, it was no log; it was something else entirely. As it got closer, Paul was both astonished and horrified to see a large "dark brown and black-colored" eel or snake-like creature—possibly ten feet in length or a little bit more—moving slowly in the water, with its head that "looked like a black sheep" flicking rapidly from side to side.

Although he had an old Polaroid camera with him, said Paul, he never even thought to take a photograph. Instead, he merely stared in both awe and shock as the animal cruised leisurely and blissfully past him before finally vanishing out of sight. Paul stressed that the creature apparently did not see him ("or, if it did, it never attacked me") and did not appear to exhibit any outright hostile tendencies.

What elevated Paul's story to a far stranger level was the fact that he claimed, in quite matter-of-fact fashion, that the following Saturday he was fishing in practically the same spot when he had a sudden, out-of-the-blue feeling of being watched. He was not wrong. Peering across the width of the canal, Paul was both horrified and petrified to see a dark, hairy face staring intently at him out of the thick, green bushes. The head of the animal was unmistakably human-like, said Paul, who added that "as soon as it saw me looking at it, up it went and ran right into the trees, and I lost it." He further explained, "That was it; a second or two was all at the most. But as it got up and ran, I knew it was a big monkey. There's nothing else it could have been. But what flummoxed me more than seeing it, though, was what was it doing there?"

A similar story in the United Kingdom can be found—a story which further reinforces the shapeshifting angle.

A woman called Eileen told me how a friend of hers named Janice underwent, decades ago, some sort of very traumatic, late-night encounter with a British man-beast in the picturesque English village of Child's Ercall. Found in North Shropshire, Child's Ercall has origins that date right back to Celtic times, and its church, St. Michael's, to the twelfth century. But, in all of its many years, the village surely never before—and maybe never since, too—encountered such a strange beast as that in the tale told to Eileen by her childhood best friend. So the story went, it was back in 1971, and Janice was fifteen at the time and living in a nearby village. Something abominable was about ready to radically upset the usual tranquil calm of old Child's Ercall.

After an evening spent with her then-boyfriend at the home of his parents in Child's Ercall, Janice was happily riding her pedal bike back home when she was shocked to see a large, hairy animal dash across the road directly in front of her, simultaneously glaring at her in a distinctly menacing fashion. Eileen recalled that Janice told her that the animal was no more than forty feet in front of her, was human-like in shape, was covered in long, flowing dark hair, possessed a pair of bright yellow eyes that twinkled, and had a black-skinned and shiny face.

Rather bizarrely, the Bigfoot-style entity seen by Janice in Child's Ercall was not the only weird creature said to have inhabited this otherwise utterly normal and pleasant little English village in times past. Legend has it that centuries ago a deadly mermaid was believed by many to inhabit an old pool there. In 1893, the writer Robert Charles Hope, the source of the story, described the case as follows in his book *The Legendary Lore of the Holy Wells of England, Including Rivers, Lakes, Fountains and Springs*: "[T]here *was* a mermaid seen there *once*. It was a good while ago, before my time. I dare say it might be a hundred years ago. There were two men going to work early one morning, and they had got as far as the side of the pond in [a] field, and they saw something on the top of the water which scared them not a little."

A careful, closer look revealed that the "something" was indeed a mermaid, as Hope noted. Fearful that the mermaid might drag them down in the depths, the men backed away—almost running. When, however, they heard her soothing, inviting voice, they had a sudden turn of thought. There was clearly some kind of hypnotic mind control at work here, as the pair were said to have instantly fallen in love with the mermaid—who told the men that there existed at the bottom of the pond a veritable treasure trove of gold. If the men would only come into the water and relieve her of the gold, they could have as much of it as they liked. It seemed to be just too good to be true. It was.

The men, said Hope, carefully made their way into the water—practically up to their chins in it—and, as they did so, the mermaid headed below the water and suddenly resurfaced with a huge piece of gold, something which led one of the men to cry out, "Good

God!" It was an exclamation that caused the mermaid to scream in ear-splitting fashion, and she then vanished beneath the waters of the old pond. Neither she nor the gold was ever seen again, the inference being that, in reality, the mermaid was a malevolent shape-shifter who was doing her utmost to lure the men to their deaths when she was forced to flee at the mention of God.

Examples of United Kingdom–based cases, in which hairy humanoids have been seen in the same precise vicinities as strange water-based beasts, absolutely abound. The idea that two very different entities could inhabit the same locales seems to be so remote as to be nearly impossible. Far more likely is the scenario of these creatures being one and the same—shapeshifters.

6
DOGS OF THE PARANORMAL KIND

ACCOUNTS OF GLOWING-EYED, HUGE black hounds of an ominous and sometimes deadly kind—which can take on multiple forms—are significant parts of the story this book tells. They are among the most feared of all shapeshifters, primarily because they are linked to the realm of the dead and the afterlife.

If you think it's tough to serve a life-long jail sentence today, you may want to take a look at life in England's Newgate Prison circa the latter part of the 1500s. To say that existence was grim for those destined to die within the infamous prison would be an understatement of epic proportions. And particularly so when you're also faced with fighting off a marauding entity that is part human and part monstrous hound. But let's not get too ahead of ourselves. A bit of background on Newgate Prison is first required.

The origins of this particularly notorious jail date back to 1188, which was the year in which its huge, creaking doors were first opened. Such was the level of violence that existed in lawless England at the time that the facility was constantly being added to, specifically to cope with the ever-growing band of murderers, rapists, and thieves that came its way. In other words, business was not just good; it was positively blooming. Things remained that way until its doors were finally shut in 1902.

It was, however, in the 1500s that Newgate Prison earned its reputation as a definitive hellhole. During this period, food for the people of London was at its lowest. Malnutrition, starvation, and death were very much the order of the day. Behind the walls of Newgate, however, things were even worse. If such a thing was possible. Yes, unfortunately, it was. Old texts and manuscripts tell of nightmarish scenarios in which the starving, desperate prisoners turned on one another, literally eating each other alive in cramped, filthy cells and amid a sickening and ever-growing stench of rotting human flesh.

One of those manuscripts, written by Samuel Rowlands, has proven to be a very curious one. Its title, in quaint, old-English style, is *The Discovery of a London Monster, Called The Blacke Dogg of Newgate: Profitable for All Readers to Take Heed By*. Rowlands said that at the very height of the terrible, cannibalistic activity—which even the guards were fearful of trying to stop, lest they, too, became food for the prisoners—a huge black dog suddenly manifested in one of the larger cells, a cell that held more than a dozen criminals.

Rowlands continued that panic-filled mayhem erupted as the red-eyed, canine fiend rampaged around the room, tearing into the bodies of the emaciated prisoners, ripping away skin, and crunching down on weakened bones. When the cell turned into what looked like some ghoulish slaughterhouse and the prisoners were all quickly and violently dead, the monstrous hound suddenly vanished—as if into thin air. Word quickly got around that the supernatural killer dog was the shapeshifted form of one of the prisoners. He was a man who had been devoured by his fellow prisoners several days earlier and had returned in the form of a diabolical hound to take out his very own unique form of lethal justice.

Beware of the (Human) Dog

Of the many and varied reports that exist of shapeshifters, there is absolutely no doubt that one of the creepiest sagas of all is that which was splashed across the pages of various newspapers in the summer of 1905. It's hardly surprising that the story attracted so much attention, given that it was focused on sightings of what can only be accurately described as a beast that was half human and half dog.

The *Rake Register* newspaper published in Rake, Iowa, related the facts surrounding the strange saga on June 15. The title of its article came straight to the point: "Dog with a Human Face." And, just for good measure, the writer of the eerie article added an atmospheric subtitle: "Strange Monstrosity Seen by Many Persons in Colorado Hills—Attempt Capture in Vain." While the *Register*'s story got picked up far and wide, it was actually based upon an earlier article—specifically one that appeared in the *Pittsburgh Press* on May 3 and was titled "Strange Animal: Has an Almost Human Face and a Red Mustache." The collective accounts paint a deeply strange picture.

So the story went, for a period of several weeks, sightings had been made of the nearly unearthly beast on the hills surrounding Buena Vista, Colorado, and also along the old railroad tracks in Wildhorse, which was a station on the Colorado Midland Railway. So far as can be determined, the first encounter—or, maybe, more correctly, the first *reported* encounter—took place on a stretch of road that crossed the Arkansas River, which weaves its winding way through Kansas, Oklahoma, Arkansas, and Colorado.

The unfortunate soul who had the distinct bad luck to be in the wrong place at the wrong time was a woman, a local and rich farmer, who was having a leisurely drive across the river atop a cart pulled by her favorite horse. Upon reaching one particular bridge that spanned the river, she slowed down, puzzled by the sight of some large, unknown animal standing rigidly in the middle of the road. Her first thought was that she was looking at a large dog, wolf, or coyote. There was, however, something decidedly not right about its head. At first, due to her distance from the animal, she could see that while the body certainly resembled that of a canid, there was something strange about its face. As she got closer, despite the horse becoming decidedly reluctant to go any farther, it became all too clear why that head looked so abnormal.

To her horror, the woman could see that, yes, the body was very dog-like. But, it was clearly no dog. Nor was it a wolf or a coyote. That much is sure from her description: the animal had large black spots on its coat, was of a grayish color, and had extraordinarily long and pointed ears. Its tail seemed to be out of proportion, too. But that was not the end of it. Far from it. Things were about to get worse. Much worse.

Upon reaching the animal, which still stubbornly refused to move, she could see that its eyes were much closer than one would expect to see on a dog. Not only that, the eyes looked incredibly human-like. In fact, to her eternal terror, she could see that the whole face looked human. This was amplified by what was a large tuft of hair under its nose that eerily resembled a mustache! The woman's horse was equally terrified, almost throwing her from the cart as it fought to rear up on its back legs.

Suddenly, just as the woman thought the beast was about to launch a violent attack, the animal issued a woeful howl and headed off into the surrounding undergrowth. Just before vanishing for good, it climbed a small local peak and turned and peered ominously at the woman—perhaps, in its own wild way, warning her not to follow its tracks. For the witness, however, this was not the most traumatic part of the encounter. As the dog turned its head away from her, and while still on that same peak, it rose up onto its back limbs and stood there in a curious, swaying fashion. And it topped everything off with a loud, ear-piercing howl before dropping to all fours and heading back into the undergrowth.

It was not seen again. At least, not by the tortured witness. In the days that followed, however, a wealth of additional accounts reached the staff of the *Pittsburgh Press*, all of which suggested that the creature had made its home somewhere in the vicinity of the river—which would have made a great deal of sense. After all, the river and its environs offered cover and camouflage as well as a plentiful supply of water and small animals to feed on.

Hardly surprisingly, it was the fact that the monstrosity was half human and half beast that really caught the attention and imagination of the press of the day. Despite almost two months of coverage, the affair of the Dog-Man of the Arkansas River came to a halt as June came to a close. The creature was not seen again. There were no reports of it being shot and killed. And no farm animals were attacked—which would have been a telltale sign of a marauding predator wildly on the loose. The overriding opinion was that, with dozens of gun-toting locals scouring the area, the animal had wisely decided to exit its current environment and head off to pastures fresh and new.

So, what was this half human, half animal? The short answer is we don't know. And we probably never will—unless, of course, others of its kind still, to this very day, haunt certain stretches of the Arkansas River. A case could, perhaps, be made that the animal had a deformed face—a condition, maybe, that gave it an eerily human-like appearance. That does not, however, provide any kind of answer to how the beast could walk on its back limbs, rather than on all four. And what about that nerve-jangling howl? Taking all of this into consideration, what we are left with appears to be a series of encounters with something that bore all the hallmarks of the classic werewolf, the ultimate predatory shapeshifter.

A Horrific Hound—In Fact and Fiction

In 1902, one of the most famous, and still very much loved, novels of all time was published. We are talking about Sir Arthur Conan Doyle's classic story *The Hound of the Baskervilles*, which had previously been serialized in the pages of *The Strand Magazine* from 1901 to 1902. The book, which has been turned into numerous hit movies and television dramas, tells an adventurous and eerie story. Namely, that of Sherlock Holmes's and Dr. Watson's investigation of a murderous, supernatural black dog that haunts the perilous, foggy landscape of Dartmoor in Devon, England. The blazing-eyed beast tasks the intrepid pair to their absolute limits before finally being defeated in a dramatic, late-night confrontation on the treacherous, foggy moor.

It is, however, a little-known fact that Conan Doyle's story was directly inspired by certain real-life events and characters. The creator of Holmes and Watson was very aware that, for centuries, reports of such huge, red-eyed hounds had widely been in circulation. And wildly, too. Numerous little villages throughout the United Kingdom spoke of the deadly, paranormal dogs in their very midst. They were almost always described as shapeshifters.

Perhaps the most famous of all of the phantom hounds of old Britain are those that are said to have frequented—and that, in some cases, still frequent—the ancient roads and pathways of the English counties of Norfolk, Essex, Suffolk, and Sussex. Their names include Black Shuck, the Shug Monkey, and the Shock. The Shuck and the Shock are classic black dogs, whereas, interestingly enough, the Shug Monkey is described as a creature which can change from hound to monkey and back again.

Even their very names have intriguing origins. While some researchers consider the possibility that all the appellations had their origins in the word *shucky,* a centuries-old word that means "shaggy," others, such as monster-hunter Jonathan Downes of the Center for Fortean Zoology, offer a far more sinister theory. In his book, *Monster Hunter*, Downes suggests that Shock, Shuck, and Shug are all based on the Old English *scucca*, meaning "demon," a most apt description, to be sure. Equally of note and relevance, the phantom black dog would often appear just before or during a wild thunderstorm. All of which brings us right back to *The Hound of the Baskervilles*.

As for one of the two archvillains in Conan Doyle's book— Sir Hugo Baskerville—he was based upon an all-too-real rich and powerful Dartmoor-based squire named Richard Cabell. He was a downright unpleasant and evil man who constantly provoked fear and terror among the locals that lived on the expansive and mysterious moors. That on the dark and stormy eve of Cabell's death a huge pack of black hounds was seen charging across Dartmoor— and under the light of a full moon—demonstrates yet another link between the world of reality and that of atmospheric literature. And talking of the real world versus fiction …

In 2007, a little more than a century after *The Hound of the Baskervilles* was published in book form, the worlds of reality and fantasy crossed paths on Dartmoor in decidedly sinister and unsettling fashion. It would not be inaccurate to say in incredible fashion, too. It's a story that revolves around one Martin Whitley, a resident of

Devon and someone with a very keen knowledge of the area and the old, sprawling landscape. It was a hot, bright summer's day when Whitley was busily showing a number of American visitors around the area. All was perfectly normal until something caught his eye. Something very unusual and out of place. Something that looked like it had just leapt out of the dark imagination of Conan Doyle himself. Except this was all too real. And Whitley was no character in an old novel. It was the real deal.

At a distance of around six hundred feet, Whitley saw a large, black-colored mass moving across the moors. Having a camera with him, he focused his telephoto lens on the whatever-it-was and took a good and careful look. He was astonished to see what appeared to be a large dog. "Large," however, would be an absolute understatement, given that Whitley described the animal as being roughly the size of a pony, according to a 2007 article by BBC News. He snapped off a bunch of pictures of the beast as it prowled around the old, atmospheric landscape. That was when things got really strange. Actually, things got beyond strange: the fiendish dog began to change its shape. More correctly … it changed species. And, elevating the bizarreness, it did so more than once.

Whitley, as he stared through the lens, found himself completely baffled and more than a little disturbed, too, to see the mysterious beast take on various forms. It changed from a dog into what looked very much like a sleek and black mountain lion, from a muscular black bear to a large boar, and even to something that resembled a pony. Despite the way it looked—for a while, at least—Whitley had serious doubts that the creature was some sort of dog, chiefly due to its immense size. So what was it?

It's hardly surprising that both the local and the national media had an absolute field day with the story when it broke. It was this huge coverage which prompted a local woman named Lucinda Reid to state that in all probability the morphing monster was actually her huge, black-coated pet Newfoundland dog, Troy, out on a fun, leisurely stroll! The United Kingdom's paranormal research community, however, remained highly doubtful of the possibility that gentle and genial Troy was the cause of all the fuss, chiefly because, as the photographs clearly demonstrated, the animal appeared to change its shape multiple times and in a matter of mere minutes. There was something else, too. Something that sent cold shudders up the spines of many.

The location of all the action was less than a mile from a huge slab of granite known locally as Bowerman's Nose, a place where more than a thousand years earlier infernal and highly dangerous witches held their terrible rites and rituals with sacrifices. *Human* sacrifices, that is. Notably, they were also witches that had the ability to shapeshift—most often into the forms of hares and black cats. And we are still not quite done. Nearby Wistman's Woods have for centuries been the rumored territory of a pack of supernatural dogs known as the Wisht Hounds. Add all those strange components together and what we have is a modern-day incarnation of a beast that many are more than content to keep relegated to the world of folklore and times long gone. And, specifically in relation to playful Troy the dog, to mistaken identity, too.

Sometimes, however, as this particularly uncanny saga graphically demonstrates, truth is not just stranger than fiction. At times, incredibly, they just might be one and the very same. And right in the heart of the twenty-first century. The ways and traditions of old are still among us, it seems.

Latin America's Nightmarish Hounds

While there is no doubt that the Phantom Black Dog is perceived as largely being a British phenomenon, it's a fact that the phenomenon of these strange creatures extends right into the heart of Latin America. We know this largely as a result of the sterling work in this area of a man named Simon Burchell. His research has shown that not only is the shapeshifting Phantom Black Dog an integral part of Latin American lore and legend, but that this specific beast eerily parallels its British cousin—in terms of both its appearance and its supernatural traits and abilities.

Indeed, in his 2007 book, *Phantom Black Dogs in Latin America,* Burchell notes that the nearly ubiquitous glowing red eyes of the beast are very often present in Latin American reports. The connections between death, disaster, and the afterlife to the beastly hounds are noted to a significant degree in Latin America, too. The Latin American version of the Phantom Black Dog also often presents itself at the likes of graveyards, certain stretches of road, and bridges. And, obviously, there is the ability of the Latin American monster to shapeshift—and even to alter its size.

Interestingly, there is one big difference between the British version and its Latin American cousin. Whereas the United Kingdom's monster does not impact to any particular degree the people of the country—aside from those who encounter it, of course—that is not the case in Latin America. Burchell's studies have shown that in some Latin American countries—and particularly so in Guatemala—the legend of the Phantom Black Dog has been utilized to influence the morals of the population. That may sound very strange, but it is absolutely true. Stories have been spread to the effect that anyone who regularly drinks alcohol might incur the wrath of a Phantom Black Dog. There is no evidence in the slightest that people who drink have a greater chance of seeing the beast, but the fear of the creature appears to have certainly influenced people to cut down on their drinking—something which the Catholic Church and its outdated morals carefully exploited.

One particular difference between the United Kingdom's hellhound and that of Latin America is that the latter is often described as having a pair of wings, something that allows it to take to the skies. As this book shows, there are more than a few shapeshifters that have the ability to fly in the air—the Mothman, of Point Pleasant, West Virginia, being a classic example.

We will give the final words on this particular matter to Simon Burchell: "Although the Black Dog may appear at first glance to be a British or north European phenomenon, it exists in essentially the same form across the entire length and breadth of the Americas. Much has been written upon the presumed Germanic, Celtic or Indio-European origin of the legend but such an origin would not explain how a highland Maya girl can meet a shape-shifting Black Dog at a Guatemalan crossroads. It appears that the Black Dog, much like the poltergeist, is a global phenomenon."

7
WITCHES AND SHAPESHIFTING

WITCHES, THEIR LEGENDARY "FAMILIARS," as they are known, and their eerie ability to disguise themselves as a variety of animals cannot be overlooked when it comes to the controversies surrounding shapeshifters. Indeed, they are an integral part of the overall phenomenon.

Warrington is a picturesque town located in the north of England and is dominated by the expansive River Mersey. Its origins date back millennia, specifically to the Roman invasion of England, which began in 43 AD. Just like so many old English towns and villages, Warrington has its very own saga of the supernatural kind attached to it. It is a story that goes back to the 1600s and revolves around the malignant machinations of a local, evil crone. She was known by the people of the area as Old Peggy Gronach and was described as being "evil, ugly and haggard." The tale is a strange one. It was carefully and independently investigated and chronicled by two English researchers of the paranormal, Neil Arnold and Wally Barnes, the former in an article titled "The Warrington Man-Beast!" and the latter in a 1990 book titled *Ghosts, Mysteries & Legends of Old Warrington.*

So the old tale goes, much-feared Peggy had for years managed to successfully stay one step ahead of the many witch-hunting gangs that roamed the countryside and were determined to see all of England's witches roasted to death on flaming bonfires. Whether due to good luck or the effects of some dark and disturbing incantation, Peggy was clearly not meant to have a fiery end. She successfully went from hamlet to hamlet and from town to town, carefully ensuring that she never—*ever*—stayed in one place for too long. And that included Warrington, too, which she chose to call her next home after skillfully eluding hunters from the eastern England city of Norwich. Although the witch-hunters failed to catch up with Peggy, her reputation most assuredly preceded her—to the effect that when word got out that *she* was on the way, a chilled and ominous atmosphere quickly descended upon Warrington and its worried people. It was an atmosphere that remained for months, to the regret of just about everyone.

Due to the fact that, back in the 1600s it took weeks—sometimes months, even—for news to travel the length and the breadth of the country, Peggy knew that she was safe for at least a while. As a result, she quickly put down roots at what became known locally as Peggy Gronach's Chicken Farm. It was a ruined, spooky old building that no one wished to visit. Not even the local, and usually adventurous, children of the town. At least, that is, not for a couple of weeks.

The day came, however, when that spirit of youthful excitement got the better of a group of young kids who decided to check out the old farm for themselves. It was something that one and all bitterly came to regret. And quickly so, too. As they stealthily crept through the wild, tall grass that surrounded an old and battered cottage that stood next to the farm, a terrible and fierce face appeared at one of the windows. The children were momentarily frozen by the sight of a creature that, with a degree of hindsight, sounds like some unholy combination of a Bigfoot and a demon: it was a hair-covered humanoid that sported blazing red eyes and two huge horns that sat on top of its large, bulbous head. Suddenly, the slavering monster was gone, and old Peggy came screaming through the front door, running wildly in the direction of the hysterical children.

When the kids told their parents of the terrible thing they had just encountered, in no time at all rumors got around that the horned, hairy thing and Peggy Gronach were one and the same—a witch that understood, and employed, the mysterious secrets of shapeshifting. And in terrible fashion. Others believed that the beast was Gronach's familiar—a supernatural entity such as an imp or a demon that could take on the form of numerous animals, such as cats, toads, rats, and monstrous things. No one dared go anywhere near the old farm, lest they became the next victim of Peggy or her familiar.

Thankfully, things quieted down for a couple of weeks. That is, until a local man pulling his horse and cart was attacked by what sounded very much like the same hideous beast. Luckily, no harm came to man nor horse, and both managed to flee the area while never looking back—an incident not unlike the one that occurred at Bridge 39 on England's Shropshire Union Canal in January 1879. Only days later, however, there was yet another supernatural assault. On this occasion, the outcome was very different: a local farmer found one of his cows savagely mutilated and killed—by violent decapitation.

Enough was now well and truly enough. A band of locals—no doubt waving flaming torches and provoking, for us, imagery of those old black-and-white *Frankenstein* movies of the 1930s and '40s—headed off to the farm. It was time to bring Peggy Gronach's reign of terror to an irreversible halt. Perhaps anticipating that she had outstayed her welcome, Peggy was nowhere in sight. Just like Elvis, she had left the building. The only telltale sign of her dark presence was the bloodied and half-eaten body of a dead goat.

Although that was the end of the story and the old hag was never seen again, years later rumors swirled around Warrington that the skeleton of a strange creature had been found semiburied in an old, nearby field. It was said to have the body of a large, four-legged animal and the skull of a human. Old, wizened Peggy struck down halfway through a terrible transformation from woman to monster? That's exactly what many of the townsfolk of Warrington thought. And who knows? Maybe they were right on the money.

Should you ever find yourself in Warrington and stumble across an old farm, it may be wise to return the way you came. And very quickly. Peggy the crone, in beastly form, may still haunt the neighborhood.

Familiars of the Witch

Within the practice of witchcraft there exists a creature that few outside of the craft will have any awareness of. It is a strange and often dangerous creature known as a familiar. When witchcraft was said to be rife across England in the 1500s and 1600s, it was widely believed that witches used small animals for a wide variety of reasons—such as spying on those who might do them harm. But, they weren't animals in the normal sense of the word. They were said to be demonic entities that possessed the ability to alter their forms into multiple kinds of animals. For the witches of the Middle Ages, the preferable forms were black cats, black dogs, hedgehogs, hares, owls, and mice.

There were very good reasons why witches would use ancient rites to invoke the presence of demonic entities that would do their bidding for them. If a witch had a grudge against a particular person, then paying that person a menacing visit would soon blow their cover and reveal them as a practitioner of the black arts—something that would typically result in them being burned alive at the stake or drowned in a nearby river. So, the cunning witch would dispatch her familiar—a demonic thing in animal form—to act on her behalf. After all, very few people would take much notice of a dog or a cat walking through the pathways of an old English village. Even fewer would likely give a hare, an owl, or a mouse a second glance. As a result, the familiar could approach the home of the targeted person, listen carefully to what was going on in the home of the person—or even place a malevolent hex upon them—and then report back to its controller.

In some cases, the demonic things that the witches called forth from their hellish realms did not take on animal form: they shapeshifted into the forms of people, something that added yet another layer to the complex matter, and nature, of the familiar. In human form, they were often easily identified by their pale skin, malevolent appearances, and dark clothes, not at all unlike the Men in Black of UFO lore—whom we will focus on later.

One might justifiably ask, at this stage, what did the familiars get out of all this? After all, Faustian pacts of this kind always require something in return. For the familiars it was blood, which often came from a sacrificed, slaughtered animal of normal proportions that the familiar would tear into and voraciously drink its blood. On other occasions, as the mythology of the era told it, the familiars would receive the blood in a very different way: they would suck it from the teat of the witch with whom they worked.

It should be stressed that, rather tragically, many women burned or drowned for being witches were actually nothing of the sort. Rather, they were elderly, single women whose only companions were pets. But, with the mindset that existed in England in the 1500s and 1600s—when the hunt for witches was at its height—any such woman might very well become the unfortunate target of hysterical, torch-wielding crowds.

So does that mean the matter of familiars has no basis in reality? No, not at all. Recall that two of the most popular guises into witch the demons would transform were black cats and black dogs. Very curious and paranormal-tinged reports of black-colored, so-called Alien Big Cats and fiery-eyed black hounds abound in the United Kingdom and continue to do so. In view of this, one might be inclined, and correct, to say that the witches and their familiars are still among us, with the ABCs and the Phantom Black Dogs still being among their favorite forms of disguise.

Changing into a Hare, Witch-Style

One animal, more than many others, that has long been associated with witchcraft, sorcery, and shapeshifting is the hare, which falls into the same family as the rabbit. They are widespread, with large populations throughout Europe, the United States, Japan, and Africa. And, on top of that, they are a most mysterious animal. When it comes to the matter of shapeshifting and hares, there's no doubt that one of the most famous cases on record revolves around a woman named Isobel Gowdie. In sharp contrast to the image that most people have of witches—namely, old, wizened hags with hooked noses—Gowdie was a young woman, a housewife from the twelfth-century Scottish village of Auldearn.

The hare, a traditional form for the shapeshifting witch.

So the story went, according to Luke Mastin in "Famous Witches—Isobel Gowdie (?–1662)" and Fiona Tinker in "Isobel Gowdie," Gowdie had secret and regular late-night meetings with the Scottish ruler of the fairies, the Queen of Elphame, as she was known—a supernatural elemental who had the ability to appear as young and beautiful woman and as an old, menacing woman. They were meetings said to have occurred deep underground, far below an ancient hill near Auldearn. They were also meetings that led Gowdie to become exposed to the secrets of shapeshifting.

Unlike so many alleged witches who suffered terribly at the hands of so-called witch-finders—who, in reality, were often merely sadistic characters who took pleasure in inflicting brutal pain and even death—Gowdie didn't have to be tortured to be convinced to spill the beans about her meetings with the fairies and her shapeshifting activities. She was wide open about her antics of the after-dark variety. She even shared with her interrogators the specific spell she used to transform herself into a hare. It went as follows:

> I shall go into a hare,
> With sorrow and sych and meickle care;
> And I shall go in the Devil's name,
> Ay while I come home again.

And, when she wished to return to human form, Gowie would mutter:

> Hare, hare,
> God send thee care.
> I am in a hare's likeness now,
> But I shall be in a woman's likeness even now.

The history books do not record Gowdie's fate; however, given the savagery of the widespread witch hunts that went on throughout England and Scotland at the time, the likelihood is that the outcome was not a positive one. Drowning or burning at the stake were the most probable outcomes for poor Isobel.

8
THE BLACK CAT PHENOMENON

THE PHENOMENON OF WERE-CATS—people who can transform themselves into cat-like creatures, and cats that have the ability to change their forms—is widespread. Tales of the creatures can be found in such diverse locations as Europe, Asia, both South and Latin America, and Africa. I have collected a number of notable cases from the United Kingdom, where I lived until 2001.

One such case, a particularly memorable and weird one, came from "James." I met him in Exeter, England, in the summer of 2001, and he is a retired fireman who encountered just such a creature on a bright, summer morning in 1978. At the time, James was living in Exwick, which is a town in the English county of Devon and is noted for its long history of encounters with Phantom Black Dogs. To what extent that is relevant is a matter of debate, but it is intriguing.

According to James, on the day in question he was out walking with his spaniel dog, Sammy, on the Haldon Hills, which provide an expansive view of the area, including the nearby city of Exeter. As James and Sammy took a pleasant walk through the hills they found themselves confronted by a very strange animal. It was Sammy who alerted James to the fact that something weird was about to go down. As the pair took their daily stroll, Sammy suddenly came to a complete halt and began to growl. It was clear she had picked up on something strange. At first, James thought that perhaps she had picked up the scent of a rabbit or a fox—although, as James admitted, Sammy had not reacted like that before when rabbits were around.

In seconds, the cause of Sammy's behavior became apparent: around fifty or sixty feet away a large black animal rose out of the deep grass. At first James assumed it was a black Labrador. It was not. In mere seconds, James realized that what was walking toward him and his faithful pet was a large black cat that resembled a mountain lion. Sammy whimpered and James's heart thumped. When the animal reached a point around twenty feet from the terrified pair, something that provoked even more terror, the huge cat rose up onto its back legs. They were legs that appeared to physically change as it transformed from a four-legged animal to a bipedal one. But that was not the weirdest part of the story.

As James looked on, pretty much frozen to the spot with fear, the face of the cat began to change and took on a malevolent, human-like appearance. A strange and sinister grin dominated the face, as the beast did nothing more than stand and stare at James and Sammy. James told me it was the terrible grin that finally made him realize that it was time to leave—as in immediately. As Sammy was only four months old at the time, it was easy for James to scoop her up under his arm and get the hell off the hills. He looked back twice: On the first occasion the cat-human was standing just as it had been thirty seconds or so earlier. On the second look, however, it was gone. By James's own admission, he and Sammy did not take another walk on the Haldon Hills for around three months.

It may not be a coincidence that in 1996, Jonathan Downes—the director of the Center for Fortean Zoology—investigated a wave of sightings of a strange, large, cat-like animal on the Haldon

Hills. Downes related the facts in his 2004 book, *Monster Hunter*. Most of the encounters occurred in the vicinity of an old pet cemetery, which housed (and still houses) the remains of numerous beloved, long-gone old friends. Downes did not solve the mystery, but he did come away from the investigation fully convinced that the Haldon Hills were home to something dangerous and predatory. James's were-cat? Don't bet against it.

An Upright Cat

A second case reached me in 2013 from "Jennifer," who lives in Oregon. Jennifer's encounter occurred in her small hometown—the name of which she prefers to keep out of the story—in the fall of 2011. It was late on a Friday night, and Jennifer had been hanging out with an old girlfriend whom she had not seen for a few months. Laughs and a few drinks were the order of the night. The laughs were, however, destined to come to a sudden, shuddering end. It was not long after midnight that Jennifer left her friend's apartment. And although the two had not seen each other for several months, they only lived approximately a ten-minute walk from each other—the lack of contact having been due to the fact that her friend had been on a temporary work assignment in Florida. So, given the close proximity to Jennifer's apartment, she decided to take a walk home, the quiet town hardly being a hotbed of crime or muggings.

Only a couple of minutes before she reached her own abode, Jennifer saw what she assumed was a large black dog walking toward her on the sidewalk—an assumption identical to the experience of James back in 1978 on the Haldon Hills. As the creature got closer, Jennifer was horrified to see it was actually a significantly sized cat. As in the size of a jaguar. Jennifer was about to make a run for cover—but to where, at that time of night, she admitted she had no idea—when the cat suddenly stood upright, changed its appearance, ran across the road at a phenomenal speed, and vanished into an alley on the other side of the road. Notably, Jennifer said that the cat did not lose its black color as it changed into human form—nor did it lose its cat-like head. It was, according to Jennifer, something that appeared half human and half cat. A definitive were-cat.

The Lairs of the Leopard Men

Within the huge continent of Africa—which covers more than eleven and a half million square miles—tales of violent and deadly so-called Leopard Men abound. It is, however, within West Africa's Sierra Leone and Nigeria that the phenomenon really dominates. It's important to note that for the people of the area, the leopard has long been perceived as a revered and feared entity. For the most part, this comes from the fact that, according to certain African teachings, the leopard is a creature that, after its bodily death, directs the human soul into the domain of the afterlife. When the leopard comes calling, death is very rarely far behind. The leopard, those same teachings maintain, has the ability to perform such a strange act due to it being what is termed a "totem animal." Namely, a creature that can effortlessly transform itself from flesh and blood to spirit—hence, while in that same spirit state, the leopard has the ability to travel from our physical, three-dimensional world to that domain where the soul resides after death.

In a very weird, yet perhaps understandable, fashion, in certain West African belief systems the transformative nature of the leopard has led people of both Nigeria and Sierra Leone to do their absolute utmost to try and emulate the supernatural leopards. They do so by, effectively, *becoming* leopards themselves, albeit in a very strange, alternative, and even deadly, fashion. Very few people—outside of those who secretly practice it, of course—have witnessed this strange form of transformation. One who did was Pat O'Dwyer, a man who held a position of significance in the area, back in the 1930s. He told his story, in first-person fashion, in "The White Man's Grave" in *The Overseas Pensioner.*

At the time, O'Dwyer held the position of Assistant District Commissioner in Port Loko, which is located in northern Sierra Leone. For the most part, O'Dwyer's job was routine and bureaucratic, but there were exceptions—extremely disturbing ones, too. On one particular day, the rotting and putrid corpse of a slain man was brought to Port Loko, having been found in a backstreet in Makeni, a major city in Sierra Leone. "Slain" barely began to describe the situation, however. The unfortunate soul was torn to pieces—something that was evident from the large claw marks that covered his body. The chief of the tribe to which the dead man belonged sent a messenger with the body—a messenger who told O'Dwyer that this was a case of cold-blooded murder. And murder at the hands of a secret society that worshipped leopards of both the physical and the supernatural variety.

Despite strongly doubting the murder theory—the claw marks were a clincher; at least for a while—O'Dwyer quickly contacted a local doctor who, in turn, equally quickly performed an autopsy. There was no doubt that the violent cuts to the body, coupled with the massive, attendant blood loss, were the causes of death. But who was the culprit? Or, maybe, *what* was the culprit? While the doctor couldn't rule out the possibility of someone having mimicked the attack of a leopard, such was the decaying state of the body—which had been left outside in the African heat for more than a day before reaching O'Dwyer—that it was hard to say anything definitive at all. It was down to O'Dwyer to try and reach a conclusion. And he did exactly that by suggesting the killer was indeed a leopard. O'Dwyer's conclusion was understandable: the man was a farmer whose farm backed onto a large area of dense forest that was known to be the home and hunting grounds of numerous savage leopards. He had, then, unfortunately been in the wrong place at the wrong time. That, however, was not the end of the story. As it transpires, it had scarcely gotten started.

When word got around that the death of the man had been relegated to the attack of a leopard—and nothing more—O'Dwyer was quietly contacted by various people in the Makeni Court who had much to say on the matter—all of it filled with controversy and menace. They suggested that while O'Dwyer was not exactly on the *wrong* track, he was certainly not on the *right* track, either. Puzzled, O'Dwyer asked what they meant. Their answers both shocked and amazed him.

In no time at all, O'Dwyer was introduced to the world of the Leopard Society. It was a murderous group that—as a result of its worship of the totem-style leopard—mimicked leopards by *becoming* them. In a very weird way, too. The group would take the skins of slaughtered leopards, stitch them together, and then wear them as one would clothes. But the transformation didn't end there. They created vicious-looking claws out of steel, which they would attach to their hands—and even to their feet—and then attack their victims in horrific, homicidal fashion.

According to Dwyer's sources, the murdered individual was not chosen at random: a great deal of planning went into the matter of determining who would become the sacrificial victim of the Leopard Society. Then, when chosen, the person would be torn to pieces by the *Bati Yeli*, none other than the executioner, who made expert use of those razor-sharp, steel claws.

The secret cult went one step further—a step that most of us would never, ever take. They engaged in full-blown cannibalism, drinking blood and eating the internal organs. This was not done out of hunger, however. Rather, the group members' primary action was to boil the intestines, creating a gruesome cocktail in the process. It was called *Borfima* and—it was widely believed—it gave them the ability to shapeshift into … of course … leopards. There was another aspect to this issue, too: namely, that ingesting Borfima would also permit a person's mind to enter that of a leopard, thus taking control of the animal's character and personality, too.

So, what we have here is a complicated situation with allegedly real shapeshifting, people supernaturally taking control of the minds of leopards, and tribespeople dressing and disguising themselves as leopards and acting out deadly rituals and killings to appease their leopard gods. And the weird story is not quite over.

As O'Dwyer looked further into this issue and gained the confidence of more and more of the people of Port Loko, he learned of other, very similar cults whose actions revolved around shapeshifting. They, too, required the drinking of human blood and the eating of the intestines as a means to allow the shapeshifting process to proceed. However, these additional cults worshipped not leopards but baboons, tigers, lions, and even alligators, animals that the followers believed they could transform into, given the right conditions and providing one followed the occult-driven rites to a tee.

Pat O'Dwyer was not the only person who spoke out on such mysterious matters. Another man who did likewise was Dr. Werner Junge, whose account is told in his book *African Jungle Doctor*, which was published in 1953. He was German but spent a great deal of time in Liberia, a country on the West Coast of Africa. In 1933, while in Liberia, Junge had the distinct misfortune to come across the body of a teenage girl who had been mutilated and killed in terrible fashion. Word soon got around that she was the victim of the Leopard Society, who had killed her and partially devoured her as a means to achieve the ability to shapeshift.

According to Junge, the girl's neck was all but destroyed, her pelvis was shattered, her intestines were gone, and one of her thighs was torn out. It was Junge's initial thought that a wild leopard was the culprit. The closer he looked, however, the more he realized that some of the slashing to the girl's body did not resemble the attack of a wild animal. They were more like the work of some sort of weapon—such as something metallic fashioned into claws—which accorded very closely with the findings of Pat O'Dwyer. And also just like O'Dwyer, Junge soon came to realize that in certain portions of Africa as late as the 1930s, belief in shapeshifting was not only widespread; it was also provoking cold-blooded murder on a significant scale.

From a Large Black Cat to a Hairy Man-Beast

On December 10, 2009, in an article titled "Cleadon BHM" paranormal investigator Mike Hallowell told of how several days earlier he spoke with a friend and research colleague, John Triplow, who informed Mike of a website that contained "an intriguing BHM [Big Hairy Man] story, not unlike that of the infamous Beast of Bolam Lake, which I actively investigated with a CFZ team in early 2003." Bolam Lake in Northumberland, England is the site of a Bigfoot-type creature seen in January 2003 by a team from the Britain-based Center for Fortean Zoology, one of the few full-time monster-hunting groups in the world.

What puzzled John Triplow—and also deeply flummoxed Mike Hallowell—was that this particular sighting of a large, hairy man-beast allegedly occurred right in the heart of Cleadon village, in the very same year that a large black cat was reportedly prowling, in sinister and similar fashion, around the neighborhood. As for why it so flummoxed Hallowell, let's take a good and close look.

Hallowell noted, quite correctly, that the Borough of South Tyneside is the smallest Metropolitan Borough in the United Kingdom, and it comprises only half a dozen villages and towns, a handful of farms, and, if one is brutally honest, not much else at all. Aside, that is, from one thing. And it's a very significant thing, too. The area, Mike revealed, was a veritable beacon for an absolute plethora of bizarre activity. That activity included ghostly experiences, UFO sightings, two Man in Black encounters, and a confrontation with a strange beast that resembled the infamous Mothman of Point Pleasant, West Virginia, which was made famous in John Keel's acclaimed book, *The Mothman Prophecies*.

As for the story of the Cleadon man-beast, Hallowell said that the witness in question reported seeing in the darkness of the night in question (a night whose precise date has yet to be ascertained) what appeared to be a large, two-legged animal covered in a thick coat of fur. A second individual was there, too—but this one undeniably human—apparently out walking their pet dog. Hallowell added that "it seemed more than a little odd to me that this BHM sighting should occur in the same village that had only a short while previously been the setting for the infamous Cleadon Big Cat incident. Two spectacular cryptids in the one village, only a few short years apart?"

It was a most puzzling question to be sure, and one that Hallowell dug into further as he attempted to resolve the nature of what, exactly, was afoot. As Hallowell began to ask more and more questions, he discovered something amazing. Namely, that both the encounter involving the large black cat and that which revolved around what might be termed a British Bigfoot occurred on the

Cleadon Hills and had witnesses out walking their dogs late at night. This gave rise to several people suspecting that the black cat and the man-beast were one and the same—a nightmarish thing that had taken on multiple grisly forms.

9
BIGFOOT AND MYSTERIOUS APES

IT MAY COME AS a surprise to many to learn that one of the world's most famous monsters—Bigfoot of the Pacific Northwest and elsewhere—is a shapeshifter. As controversial as it may sound, reports of strange, unidentified apes that have the ability to take on numerous guises—all around the planet, never mind just in the United States—abound.

There is absolutely no doubt that Rendlesham Forest, in the English county of Suffolk, is most famous for a series of sensational UFO encounters that occurred across the period of December 26–29, 1980. Multiple military personnel from the nearby twin bases of Royal Air Force Benwaters and Royal Air Force Woodbridge reported seeing strange lights in the sky. Their accounts can be found in an official US Air Force document of January 13, 1981, titled "Unexplained Lights." It was written by Lieutenant Colonel Charles I. Halt, the Deputy Base Commander at Bentwaters. Other saw UFOs beaming lights down to the weapons storage areas—which were the secret home to nuclear weapons. There are even accounts of some of the airmen seeing small, humanoid figures with cat-like eyes—aliens, perhaps. It's a far less known fact, however, that Rendlesham Forest has its very own shapeshifter. Its name is the Shug Monkey. Like most shapeshifters, it is a creature that terrifies all those who encounter it.

"Sam Holland," whom I spoke with in 2001, encountered the Shug Monkey as he walked his little dog through the woods back in 1956. Holland described the monster as a veritable chimera: part monkey, part dog, and part bear. That it had a length of around ten feet demonstrates it was no normal, or even known, animal. Fortunately, neither Holland nor Harry the dog were harmed by the lumbering creature, which, after briefly glaring at the petrified pair, vanished into the woods.

A near-identical animal was seen seven years later in the same stretch of forest by a woman named Peggy Cushing; the only difference—a very significant difference—being that the animal suddenly changed into the form of a hideous, bat-winged gargoyle, and which soared off into the dark skies above! Notably, Cushing said that as the beast changed in shape, there was a shimmering effect surrounding it.

Adding yet another component to the story is an account that comes from monster hunter Jonathan Downes. He is the director of the Center for Fortean Zoology and someone who accompanied me on my 2004 expedition to Puerto Rico in search of the legendary chupacabra, a story I told in my 2015 book, *Chupacabra Road Trip*. Downes described, in his 2008 book, *Island of Paradise*, how in 1996 an old girlfriend of his had shown him a very interesting piece of film footage of unidentified paw prints found in a certain area of muddy ground in Rendlesham Forest, a year or two earlier. They closely resembled the prints of a cat, but of what variety no one could say. What could be said, however, is that they were far bigger than the kinds of prints that would be left by even the largest lion, tiger, or leopard. Of course, there is nothing roaming the wilds of the United Kingdom of such a size. Or, at least, there shouldn't be any such beast on the loose. There have, how-ever, been multiple encounters in Rendlesham Forest with what have become known as "Alien Big Cats," or ABCs, but not even they can boast of being the size of the animal that left the prints studied by Jonathan Downes.

Moving on, we have the account of "Tom Potter," a local man who was witness to a large monkey-like animal seen in Woodbridge in the early hours of a 1987 morning. I met Potter in December 2000, and right in the heart of Rendlesham Forest, when a twentieth anniversary party to celebrate the 1980 UFO landing was held there. As Potter drove to work at around 4:30 a.m. and passed the fringes of Rendlesham Forest, he caught sight of a creature that was not dissimilar to a chimpanzee. In fact, that is exactly what he thought the creature was as he slowed his vehicle to a near-halt and watched it amble along the road at a leisurely pace. That is, until it suddenly stopped and turned to look at Potter, whose vehicle was moving at a speed of barely a couple of miles per hour at the time. According to Potter, the "chimpanzee" dropped onto its four limbs, was briefly lit up by a white light, and took on the form of a sleek and shiny black cat. It then suddenly raced into a nearby field and was not seen again.

The idea that Rendlesham Forest could be home to numerous unknown animals—such as Sam Holland's ten-foot-long beast, Tom Potter's "chimp-cat," and Peggy Cushing's nightmarish gar-goyle—is absurd. In all likelihood, and particularly so when one takes into consideration the testimony of Cushing and Potter, we are dealing with a creature that is not limited to one physical form. A supernatural chimera, one might justifiably suggest.

An intriguing and thought-provoking afterword: With multi-ple animal forms seen roaming around Rendlesham Forest—and for decades—what does all of the above say about the famous UFO encounter of late December 1980? While it is not impossible that extraterrestrials from a faraway star system may have touched down in the woods all those years ago, the more logical answer to the riddle is that the UFO events were *also* the result of shapeshifting, but on this occasion the phenomenon chose to take on the form of ET. Which begs an even more thought-provoking question: What form will the shapeshifting intelligence of Rendlesham Forest turn into next?

A Ghost-Filled Road

Encounters with mysterious, glowing balls of light, ones that have the mystifying ability to change into the forms of strange and savage creatures, are not unknown in the United States: it's far from being a solely British phenomenon. A classic example is the large body of data that surrounds a certain huge area of forest in Texas. As someone who is proud to call the Dallas–Fort Worth area his home, I am all too well aware that many people think and assume that Texas is just one big desert. In reality, however, that's far from the case. Yes, West Texas is extremely flat and filled with almost endless fields of cotton. And, it's also true that South Texas has its fair share of harsh and scalding landscapes. However, Central, North, and East Texas are very different: they are dominated by thick forestland that extends for miles and miles … and miles. Indeed, a 2011 Forest Inventory and Analysis report prepared by the Texas Forest Service revealed that Texas's woods ran to 62.4 million acres and cover almost 40 percent of the state. And it's to one particular area of dense woodland that we have to turn our attention. Its name: the Big Thicket.

The late Rob Riggs in the Big Thicket.

Located in the Piney Woods area of East Texas, the Big Thicket has a most apt moniker: it is a huge, 83,000-acre area of woodland. "Dense" barely begins to describe the massive, forested environment, which is home to numerous wild animals, including alligators and bobcats, as well as other creatures of a very odd kind, as we'll soon see. Running through the heart of the Big Thicket is a long, thin, and incredibly sandy old road called Bragg Road. That's not what the locals call it, though. To them, it is known as Ghost Light Road. There is a very good reason for this: for at least three centuries, people have reported seeing weird, small balls of light flitting through the trees late at night. But, we're not talking about anything quite as down to earth as fireflies. These particular lights vary in size from—approximately—a tennis ball to a beach ball. They also exhibit evidence of intelligence: witnesses describe the lights approaching them, even circling them, in what is occasionally perceived as a playful fashion. Such is the interest the lights provoke in the people that live there, and in visitors too, that a historical marker has been erected at the start of Bragg Road and details the strange story of the lights.

The late Rob Riggs was one of the most learned figures in the Bigfoot research field and someone who spent a significant portion of his life living in the Big Thicket area. Riggs collected numerous reports of the mysterious ghost lights, dating back to the 1800s. But Riggs did far more than that. He also catalogued an astonishing number of reports of what seemed to be Bigfoot and large, black leopards. I say "seemed to be" for a very good reason.

Of the people who have reported seeing large black cats or have had hairy wild-man–type encounters in the Big Thicket, the vast majority are content to conclude they encountered animals of the type that very few ever get to encounter. But, not all of them. A small body of individuals has sworn that the large cats and the hairy humanoids—when spotted by these astonished and sometimes terrified onlookers—vanished before their eyes. We're not talking about them making hasty getaways into the woods. Rather, we are talking about the "animals"—in an instant—changing form from big cat and Bigfoot to a small, brightly lit globe of light. The ghost lights have been staple parts of the area for centuries, of course.

Three such reports surfaced in 1977 from entirely unconnected people: two encountered the Big Thicket man-beast, and one the paranormal panther. All three witnesses—whose accounts were collected by Ernie Sears, a now-deceased UFO researcher, swore that, in barely a couple of blinks of the eye, and as the creatures realized they had been seen, they became as still as statues. Then, rather incredibly, they shrunk in size and transformed into small balls of light that vanished into the trees.

The Lone Star State's infamous Ghost Road.

A nearly identical incident occurred on Bragg Road itself in 1998, when a group of campers encountered an immense Bigfoot—in excess of eight feet in height—which vanished in a flash of light and that left just one telltale card: a golf ball–sized globe of light that hovered around the immediate area for around twenty or thirty seconds and then fizzled out of existence, amid what was described as an electrical crackling noise. I had the good fortune to meet one of the campers at the June 11, 2005, Texas Ghost Lights Conference in Austin, Texas.

Finally, in 2007, one of the mysterious big cats was seen by a wildlife officer as it drank from a small pool of water deep in the Thicket. The woman—whom I met on a 2009 trip to the Big Thicket and who prefers anonymity—knew all the stories of the area's resident "black panther" but didn't really put much faith in the accounts. That is, until she saw it for herself. And she saw much more than that: as she stood transfixed to the spot, the immense cat turned nonchalantly in her direction and was suddenly reduced to a glowing ball that melted into the pool amid a great deal of steam, suggesting the light was extremely hot.

In view of all the above, it's no wonder that the Big Thicket has developed a reputation as one of the most paranormal places in all of the Lone Star State.

10
DANGEROUS MIMICS

MOST SHAPESHIFTING MONSTERS SEEM to be content with terrifying and tormenting us. But not all of them. Some of these creatures are deeply cunning and are intent on luring us into their nightmarish realms, quite possibly to try and take our lives. Maybe even our souls, too.

Aside from literal shapeshifting, there is another, related aspect to the mystery that is downright eerie and menacing in the extreme. It is the ability of certain monsters—and almost always Bigfoot-type creatures—to very closely mimic us. And, specifically, to mimic the stress-filled cries of babies. As the following accounts collectively demonstrate, the clear implication is that the beasts mimic the vocalizations of babies in distress as a means to lure us into their environments. To attack or kidnap us? To kill us? Maybe even to savagely devour us? The questions are many. They are deeply chilling questions, too.

Bigfoot comes to Texas.

The small town of Ennis, Texas, was the site of a brief series of such encounters with a Bigfoot-style entity in 1964. Those same encounters involved an immense monster, one which was described by the half a dozen people who saw it as being somewhere between eight and ten feet in height. It is a saga told by the Bigfoot Research Organization in an article titled "Tall Creature Seen by Witness." Notably, nearly all the encounters occurred at the site of an old, and now-demolished, wooden bridge that spanned the still-existing Chambers Creek. Eye-opening is the fact that the bridge became known by the locals as Cry-Baby Bridge—on account of the disturbing, and baby-like wailings that were always heard when the hairy monster was around. Fortunately, despite the voice *sounding* like the cries of a baby, no one fell for the potentially deadly ruse. All recognized it for what it was: an attempt to reel in the witnesses but for reasons that remain unknown. They were surely nothing of a positive nature.

Five years later, in 1969, the Ennis Bigfoot was back again—as were the baby-like cries, which continued to haunt the old bridge and those who saw the beast across what was a period of roughly five weeks. Again, the monster was immense: around nine feet tall. There was a difference, however: the Bigfoot was seen to run on both four limbs and two, despite looking entirely humanoid in shape and stance when upright. That it was able to race through the trees in dog-like fashion—and in human-like fashion, too—strongly suggests that a fair degree of shapeshifting was afoot.

The Cryer Creek Cemetery.

One final thing on this particular matter: of the several old graveyards that can be found in and around the Ennis area, one is called Cryer Creek Cemetery. Cryer Creek is a town located just a few miles from Barry, Texas. Today, it has a population of less than twenty. That's to say the dead significantly outnumber the living in the nineteenth-century town. There is a notable story behind the name of the town.

When it was settled in the 1850s by one William Melton, one of the most important things on the agenda was the name of the town. It is eye-opening to note that the name chosen, Cryer Creek, was inspired by local legends. They were legends that suggested if one were to walk the old, nearby creeks late at night, one would hear the fear-filled cries of a woman. That there are stories of strange cries amid the local creeks dating back to the middle years of the nineteenth century strongly suggests that Chambers Creek's monstrous mimics were around long before the events of 1964 began.

Now, let's take a trip to the 1970s.

Stan Gordon, a chronicler of the stranger side of the Bigfoot enigma.

The UFO Connection

Stan Gordon is one of the world's leading figures in the field of Bigfoot investigations—and particularly cases that are steeped in mystifying high-strangeness. In October 1973, Gordon investigated a very weird case focused on the late-night landing of a brightly lit UFO in a rural part of Pennsylvania; it's a case that appears in Gordon's 2010 book, *Silent Invasion*. As a group of concerned and inquisitive locals reached the area of farmland where the UFO touched down, the air was filled with the sound of what seemed to be—yes, you guessed right—a crying baby.

As the group got closer, they could see a significantly sized dome-like object sitting in the darkness of a large pasture. If that was not enough, to the horror of the men a pair of large and lumbering Bigfoot loomed out of the shadows and proceeded to head toward them. Panic immediately erupted, and the group scattered, firing their guns at the beasts as they did so. The bullets had no effect, and no evidence of a baby—in distress or otherwise—was ever found. Of course, their concern for the baby was the key thing that spurred them on to close in on the UFO. Which, in all likelihood, was the goal of the sly, mimicking monsters in their midst.

Meanwhile …

Back to a Certain Bridge

Bob Carroll, whom I chatted with at the October 1996 Staffordshire UFO Conference in Cannock, England, had a very similar encounter in January or February of either 1972 or 1973 at Bridge 39 on England's Shropshire Union Canal, the very same location that spawned the diabolical Man-Monkey in January 1879, as we have already seen. It was the early hours of the morning and Carroll, a truck driver, was driving to the nearby town of Newport, where he was due to make a 6:00 a.m. delivery, having picked up a pallet of paint from a depot in the city of Leicester the previous evening. Everything was completely normal until he approached ... yes ... that damned bridge.

Stressing that everything was over in a few seconds, Carroll said that it was his natural instinct to slow down as he reached the bridge. As he did so, he was shocked to see from his cab a hair-covered humanoid race out of the trees, cross the bridge, and head down to the old canal. Carroll was amazed by the incredible speed and apparent agility of the beast as it bounded across the road and was subsequently, and quickly, lost to sight. He estimated that its height was four and a half to five feet at the very most, that it had dark fur, and that it looked very muscular. Stressing that he had always been a gung-ho type, Carroll quickly pulled over to the side of the road, turned on the hazard lights of his truck, and ran back to the scene of his bizarre and brief experience.

On reaching the canal bridge, Carroll quickly peered over both sides; however, the total lack of light made any attempt to see much of anything tangible nigh on impossible. But there *was* one other odd thing that Carroll was keen to relate, something that, by now, will be as familiar as it is disturbing. As he leaned over the bridge, he heard what he was absolutely sure were ... the loud and distressing cries of a baby. In fact, he said the cries were *too* loud—almost ear-splitting and echoing. Despite feeling that he needed to help the "baby," Carroll nearly immediately developed a feeling that this was no baby. Rather, he felt, it was the monkey-like animal, ingeniously and cunningly trying to lure him down to the canal for an encounter of the fatal kind.

Carroll, probably very wisely, did not act upon the beast's macabre ruse. It may very well have been a decision that saved his life.

Otter-Men of Alaska

The Kushtaka—or the Kooshdakhaa, as it is also known—is a monstrous, manipulative, and sometimes deadly creature that is a staple part of the folklore of two specific groups of Native Americans living predominantly in the state of Alaska but also in other portions of the Pacific Northwest Coast. Their names are the Tsimshian and the Tlingit. The former are known as the "People of the Tides," while the latter are referred to as being "Inside the Skeena River," on account of the fact that they once inhabited significant portions of the Skeena River in British Columbia. It is within the teachings of these two tribes of people that we learn of the hideous shapeshifting things that provoke mayhem, terror, and death throughout the region.

Dennis Waller is one of the leading experts in the field of the Kushtaka. He notes in his 2014 book, *In Search of the Kushtaka*, that the word *Kushtaka* equates to "Land Otter Man," which is highly appropriate taking into consideration that this is precisely how the Kushtaka is described. It is important, however, to note that the creature is not literally half human and half otter. Rather, it can take on both forms. But things don't end there: the Kushtaka can also manifest in the shapes of giant wolves—very often bipedal, upright wolves—and also large, hairy humanoids not at all unlike Bigfoot. In the Bigfoot-seeking community, Waller observes, this has given rise to the thought-provoking theory that the Kushtaka may well be an Alaskan Bigfoot, one that, over time, has been incorporated into Native lore and legend. On the other hand, however, and as Waller also notes, for the Tsimshian and the Tlingit, the creatures are monsters with the power to morph. In that sense, the jury is very much out when it comes to their true identities.

Dennis Waller, an expert on the shapeshifting Kushtaka.

The otter angle is a very intriguing one and is born out of the fact that otters are highly intelligent animals, that they have structured communities and even leaderships, that they are occasional tool users, and that they even hold each other's hands. These parallels—between the societies and actions of both otters and humans—amount to one of the key issues that led the Tsimshian and Tlingit people to associate them in very much the same fashion. There is, however, yet another aspect to the otter issue.

Otters are perceived as being good-natured and friendly animals—which, for the most part, they certainly are. But not for the two tribes that fear the Kushtaka. For the tribespeople, the engaging and outward character of the otter is merely a ruse, one that is designed to deceive and manipulate people and to lure them into situations that range from the stressful to the outright deadly. Notably, tribal history maintains that each and every otter is secretly part human, something that allows it to jump from form to form as it sees fit.

It is very eye-opening to learn that the Kushtaka has a notable way of luring its human prey into darkened forests, where it can work its evil ways: it mimics the cry of a baby, or that of a young child, in distress. As we have seen, such similar, cunning activity has been reported in Bigfoot encounters in Texas, Pennsylvania, and also at Bridge 39 on England's Shropshire Union Canal, the home of the hair-covered shapeshifter known as the Man-Monkey. Clearly, there is an undeniable connection here—a connection that is made all the more fascinating by the fact that these stories span not just countries but even entire continents. This begs an important question: How could such tales proliferate centuries ago and from lands separated by thousands of miles? Coincidence? Doubtful. Far more likely, the people of those widely varied areas and eras encountered extremely similar shapeshifters, ones that utilized the very same supernatural skills, mimicry, and powers.

One of the primary activities of the Kushtaka is to steal the soul—or the supernatural essence—of its targeted victim. This, too, is something that we have seen before, and specifically in relation to shapeshifters. When a tribesperson loses his or her soul, it is the responsibility of the tribe's medicine man—or shaman—to seek out the specific Kushtaka that made its victim definitively soulless and to then hopefully wrestle it from the Kushtaka and reunite body and soul into one. And, just like the water-based selkies of Scotland's Shetland Islands—creatures that we will address later—the Kushtaka is known for its cunning and callous ability to lure sailors to watery graves, deep below the high seas. Oddly, despite its malignant and dangerous reputation, the Kushtaka is sometimes helpful—even to the extent of saving someone in dire peril. This parallels the tales of shapeshifting fairies. It should be noted, however, that such positive cases are very much few and far between.

Although the vast majority of all reports of the Kushtaka come from the Tlingit and the Tsimshian people, that is not exclusively the case. A particularly spine-tingling story, dating from 1900, came from *The Strangest Story Ever Told* by the late Harry D. Colp.

Colp was an adventurer, gold prospector, and someone who firmly believed that he encountered a colony of Kushtaka at Thomas Bay, which is located in the southeastern part of Alaska. It is also known as the Bay of Death, as a result of a huge land-fall that occurred at the bay in the mid-eighteenth century. Its far more chilling name, however, is Devil's Country, on account of the Kushtaka legends and encounters.

According to Colp, as he climbed one particular ridge one day, he developed a sudden sense of being watched. As Colp quickly turned around, he was terrified to see an entire group of horrif-ic-looking monsters carefully and diligently pursuing him. In eye-opening fashion he described them as creatures that appeared to be half human and half monkey. He also described them as be-ing sexless, suggesting, in all probability, that he meant no genitalia was seen. This is not at all surprising, as Colp said that the entire pack was covered by long and thick hair—aside from those areas covered by oozing, infected sores. As the monsters moved closer and closer, howling and screaming in the process, Colp wretched at the foul odor that emanated from their forms—to the point where he almost passed out. Fortunately, after hurling his broken rifle at them, Colp managed to outrun his hideous pursuers, ensuring that he did not fall victim to this grisly band of hungry beasts.

There is no doubt at all that the tale of Harry D. Colp has more than a few Bigfoot-themed overtones attached to it: the strange howling, the stinking smell, and the description of the animals appearing to be semihuman and semimonkey are all part and parcel of what, today, passes for much of Bigfoot lore. Add to that the aforementioned ability of the Kushtaka to imitate the stressed cries of a baby—just as Bigfoot does—and what we have is an undeniable connection. That the Tlingit and the Tsimshian people are firmly of the belief that the Kushtaka is a shapeshifter, however, suggests something potentially mind-blowing: Bigfoot may well not be the flesh and blood beast that so many cryptozoologists believe it to be. It, too, may have the ability to morph into multiple forms—and all of them monstrous.

Such theories are not at all popular within the Bigfoot-seeking community, with many seekers of the truth preferring to conclude that the creatures may represent relic populations of *Gigantopithecus*. It was a huge ape that roamed around China, the Himalayas, and India hundreds of thousands of years ago but is generally accepted as having become extinct in the distant past. Nevertheless, the shapeshifting issue has at least been addressed by that same community, as the Oregon Bigfoot group notes in their article, "What Is Bigfoot?": "Some witnesses believe they have documented trackways that simply stop, leading some to wonder if Bigfoot may be 'interdimensional'—whatever that means—or have the ability to 'shapeshift' into another form. Some witnesses have indicated that Bigfoot can 'turn into' a rock or a stump or become invisible."

11
BLINDED BY THE LIGHT

ALL THE SHAPESHIFTERS DETAILED in this book are strange; there is no doubt about that. Perhaps the strangest of all, however, is a certain entity that appears to be purely energy based: a ball of glowing light that possesses a high degree of intelligence and can change itself as it sees fit.

It's very seldom that we find evidence of shapeshifters within the pages of formerly secret government files. On occasion, however, such an extraordinary thing does occur. The year was 1962 and the location was the village of Avebury, Wiltshire, England—a village that is noted for its huge, ancient stone circle, the construction of which began around 300 BC. Avebury is both picturesque and eerie in equal measures. Such a thing is hardly surprising when one takes into consideration the fact that a trip to Avebury is almost akin to taking a trip back in time, to a period when Neolithic man dominated the land, human sacrifice to ancient gods was not unknown, and magic and mystery were all-encompassing. As we will now see, however, Avebury has managed to successfully retain that air of ancient intrigue.

Under the terms of the British Government's Freedom of Information Act, a fascinating document has surfaced, one that gives us a high degree of insight into what the world of officialdom thinks of the shapeshifter controversy. In typically bureaucratic style, the document has a decidedly nonsensational title: "Flying Saucer Incident, Avebury, Wilts., September 4, 1962." Technically speaking, the incident did have a UFO component to it, but there was more to it than that. In fact, way more—as will now become astonishingly clear.

It's first important to note that the case itself was treated with the utmost seriousness: it was not assigned to a low-level employee of the government but to senior military personnel attached to the British Royal Air Force's Provost and Security Services, whose work revolves around countering terrorism, engaging in espionage on hostile nations and organizations, and running counterintelligence and disinformation operations.

The story at issue originated with a fifty-two-year-old woman whose name—to this day—remains blacked out on the relevant, now-declassified pages of the curious dossier. What we do know, however, is that she lived in the old village and had done so for her entire life. In addition, she had a deep affinity to the old standing stones fashioned and positioned by the long-gone Neolithic people. As to how, and under what circumstances, the events that led the Royal Air Force's finest to descend upon sleepy old Avebury began, it was all due to the fact that the woman in question often walked late at night among the stones—something that, she told the officers, relaxed her and gave her a sense of comfort. Which is truly ironic: there was nothing relaxing or comforting about the terrifying encounter she was about to experience.

During the course of an interview undertaken by a pair of officers from the Provost and Security Services' Special Investigations Section, the witness explained that it was her typical habit to take a walk around the stones late at night and at least twice per week;

the dark skies and the quiet atmosphere were particularly enjoyable to her. Today, the population of Avebury is less than 600. Back in 1962, it was slightly less, something that all but guaranteed the woman would be all alone as she walked the old stone circle.

One of the mysterious standing stones of Avebury, England.

As she did so—the time, she recalled being somewhere between 10:30 p.m. and 10:45 p.m.—the woman was astonished to see a brightly illuminated, circular body of white light floating among the stones of Avebury. Moving about the grassy ground in total silence—and at a height of little more than ten feet—it appeared, she said, to be under some form of intelligent control. Her reason for thinking that was entirely reasonable: time and again, the roughly two-foot-in-diameter ball swerved around the stones, clearly being careful not to touch any of them, and then stopped right in front of her, at a distance of roughly fifteen feet. What happened next plunged the woman into a state of absolute, cold fear.

It was all she could do to stare at the light, amazed and in awe. That is, until the area was—quite out of the blue—lit up by a bright light. It was not unlike that of a camera flash, but far more powerful, to the extent that for twenty or thirty seconds her vision was severely affected. The petrified woman dropped to the ground, fearful that she would lose her balance with her vision impaired. She began to hyperventilate, such was her extreme terror, and nearly fainted as she sought to understand what was happening to her. She soon found out.

The witness stayed on all fours for a minute or several and then finally, shakily stood up. In seconds, however, relief was replaced by yet another bout of terror. The ball of light was nowhere in sight. But *something else* was. In exactly the same place where the glowing object stopped in front of her, there was now what she described to the investigating officers as a huge worm. Her description was very apt: around six feet in length and close to a foot in thickness, the pale-colored monster opened a pair of large, penetrating eyes and slowly slithered across the grass in a creepy, wormy fashion—and in her direction.

Thankfully, the woman—acting on raw and pure instinct—jumped to her feet, raced for the safety of her home, and bolted the door. She quickly dialed 999—which is the United Kingdom's equivalent of the United States' 911—and was referred to the military by the nearest police station. In an unfortunate set of circumstances, both the police and the Provost and Security Services initially failed to appreciate the seriousness of the incident and—at first, at least—wrote it off as a crank call. Until, that is, the next morning, when the P&SS representatives arrived around 9:00 a.m. and found the woman locked inside her home and utterly unwilling—or psychologically unable—to venture outside.

It was when she finally let the officers in that they realized the gravity of the situation. The woman told her story to the two men—after making one and all hot cups of tea—and agreed to accompany them to the spot where the ball of light had morphed into a monstrous worm. The beast, thankfully, was not in sight. What was in view, however, and right in front of the particular stone where the creature had appeared, was a line of an unidentified slimy substance that the officers carefully collected and deposited into a glass jar provided by the woman.

After ensuring that the woman was now okay and didn't need any medical treatment for stress, anxiety, or hyperventilation, the pair thanked her, requested in calm tones that she not talk about the event, and went on their way. She heard nothing from anyone in officialdom, at all. It is, perhaps, somewhat telling that in the declassified-but-censored files, there is no reference to what that strange slime was, even though it was surely analyzed extensively. The matter of the ball of light that shapeshifted into a vile beast sank into the dark depths of official secrecy.

As we shall see now, the Avebury affair was far from being a solitary one when it comes to the matter of balls of light morphing into other forms—some human and others downright monstrous.

Bright Lights and Fields of Frights

It's important to note that the old village of Avebury, England, is located in the county of Wiltshire. Why so? Because the fields of Wiltshire are the collective focal point for the many and varied crop circles that appear every year and that entertain the public, provoke a great deal of media coverage, and utterly entrance followers of the unexplained. Far more significant, however, is that reports have been made of strange creatures seen in crop circles and in direct association with unidentified balls of light—very much like the one seen in Avebury back in 1962 that attracted official, secret attention.

Marcus Matthews is the author of the 2007 book *Big Cats Loose in Britain*. As the title suggests, it's a book that focuses on a shape-shifting phenomenon we have already addressed in the pages of this book; namely, the so-called Alien Big Cats, or ABCs. Shortly after Matthews's book was released, he shared with me an extraordinary story. It was the story of a woman who, in the 1990s, had seen a large "black panther" (as she described it) leisurely sitting in the heart of one of the highly complex pictogram-style crop circles that appear in Wiltshire every year.

A modern day mystery: the crop circle.

When I mentioned this at one of my old blogs, *There's Something in the Woods*, it prompted three completely unconnected people who had also seen large black cats in Wiltshire-based crop formations to contact me. Of particular note, of those three, two were drawn to the specific circular creations by sudden flashes of light that caught their attention. It was as a result of the curious illumination that the witnesses found themselves heading in the direction of the formations. And, also, to what was *within* those formations: large, fierce-looking cats with glossy, black coats, huge paws, and sizeable and noticeable white fangs. It's hardly surprising that the witnesses, in both cases, fled the areas immediately. Neither chose to call the police, with one stating that it was one thing to come across a crop circle, but it was quite another to have seen a huge black cat sitting bolt upright within its confines!

Matthew Williams is someone who has played an extensive role in the crop circle enigma since the mid-1990s. Welshman Williams has investigated formations, staked out fields late at night, flown over them in his very own microlight and filmed them, and even created them. Williams, too, has had an experience that adds further weight to the theory that the mysterious balls of light of Wiltshire have the uncanny ability to transform into amazing animals and hideous beasts. In Williams's case, it all went down in the early hours of a summer morning in July 1999.

Williams explained to me that he and a friend named Paul were deep in the heart of crop circle territory when, as they stood at the fringes of a large field in which an equally large formation had been found, the pair was astounded by something wholly unanticipated. It was the sudden appearance of a trio of small balls of light hovering on the fringes of the field. At first, they were clustered together at heights of between thirty and forty feet, but then they suddenly split up and created a triangular formation, with each ball positioned around sixty feet from the others. Clearly, there was some form of orchestrated intelligence at work—which closely echoes the Avebury affair of 1962. The two men stood still for a few seconds, staring into the dark skies and at the approximately soccer ball–sized lights and wondering just what might happen next. They didn't have to wait for too long to find out.

The lights suddenly vanished at the exact time that deep and ominous growling, the distinct noises of something large and heavy crunching its way—or their way—along the field, and animal-like screams filled the chilled air. The tables had been duly turned: the crop circle investigators were now, themselves, being investigated. But by what? It was clear to Williams and Paul that whatever the creatures were, that same crunching suggested they were much bigger than the average wild English fox, which is largely a nonthreatening and even shy animal. And the screams and growls were clearly not those of foxes, either. The two men looked at each other for a moment and quickly got the hell out of Dodge, as the old saying goes.

To this day, Williams keeps an open, and serious, mind on the possibility that the trio of anomalous lights and the monstrous creatures that stalked him and Paul in that dark old field in the summer of 1999 were not just connected, but were possibly one and the very same.

12
FAIRIES AND THE LITTLE PEOPLE

GOBLINS, PIXIES, FAIRIES, THE "wee folk," and sprites all have one thing that unites them: their mystifying, magical ability to present themselves to us in a wide and varied body of ways.

W. Y. Evans-Wentz was born in Trenton, New Jersey, in 1878 and developed a deep interest in the world of the paranormal at a young age. It was an interest that he never lost. It is safe to say that it stayed with him until his death in 1965. As well as being a respected anthropologist, Evans-Wentz was someone who was also fascinated by Buddhist teachings and beliefs. In addition, he was particularly drawn to Celtic folklore and legend—the latter being an issue that is directly relevant to the theme of this book. Evans-Wentz was a prestigious writer and publisher, having published in 1927 *The Tibetan Book of the Dead,* an English version of the widely acclaimed and still extensively read *Bardo Thodol.* As for his own books, they were as notable as they were varied, one of the most revered being *The Fairy-Faith in Celtic Countries.* It's a book that is packed with fascinating accounts of old, supernatural encounters between the people of Ireland, Wales, Scotland, the Isle of Man, and Brittany and magical entities that have variously been referred to as elementals, fairies, goblins, sprites, and the "wee folk." One story collected by Evans-Wentz—and published in *The Fairy-Faith in Celtic Countries*—particularly stands out.

The tale was personally shared with Evans-Wentz by a colleague at England's Jesus College at Oxford University, a university that Evans-Wentz studied at as a young man. The story told to Evans-Wentz was as bizarre as it was undeniably sensational. Evans-Wentz knew the man well enough, however, to assert that he was no fantasist or liar. It was an account given to Evans-Wentz in 1910, just one year before *The Fairy-Faith in Celtic Countries* went to print and became a deserved classic of its kind.

The man in question was Irish and a former resident of County Kerry and had chosen Oxford University as his place of education. According to the curious story told to Evans-Wentz, it was in the first week of December 1910 that the man and a friend were heading home from a night out in the Irish city of Limerick. Given that it was a fair distance away and darkness was already on the land when they went out—never mind during their return—they chose to travel on horseback, something that would make the journey to Limerick, and home again, an easy one. It turned out, however, that fate had other things in store for the two twenty-three-year-olds. Very strange and unforgettable things.

It was as they approached Listowel—a fourteenth-century market town in County Kerry—that the men saw a powerful, brilliant light at a distance of around half a mile from them. At first, they assumed it was nothing stranger than the lights of a nearby cottage. They were wrong, however, and significantly so, too. As the pair got closer they could see that the light was not coming from a cottage, after all—or, indeed, from any kind of building. As they brought their horses to a standstill, the two could now see that the flaming light was actually floating in the air at a fairly low level. Or, in the words of Evans-Wentz's friend and colleague himself, it was "moving up and down, to and fro, diminishing to a spark, then expanding into a yellow luminous flame."

Suddenly, the light was joined by another one that was practically identical in appearance and also in size, which was somewhere in the order of around six feet in height. As the two men sat on their horses and stared in amazement at these curious displays of light, they saw something incredible happen: within the flames that were contained in the two lights, they could see a pair of what were described as radiant beings with "human form," the flames having transformed into the entities. The lights then moved toward each other and unified as one. The figures within, Evans-Wentz was told, then strode out of the lights and toward the two men. Incredibly, they seemed to be glowing. In other words, the brilliance they gave off was not a reflection from the balls of light that surrounded them. No, they were radiating the glowing eeriness themselves.

Such was the brightness that the two friends were unable to make out if their visitors of the night were male or female or one of each, but they were clearly humanoid and had noticeable halos around their heads. As far as we know—and it's unlikely that Evans-Wentz would have omitted anything from his 1911 book—the glowing entities did not utter any words, but neither of the men sensed anything malevolent about the experience. As they continued to watch in awe, and after a few minutes of silence, the glowing beings began to shrink in size and were sucked back into the balls of light, which also began to shrink—at a very fast pace. When they were barely the size of a penny, they flickered out of existence. The men stared into the now darkness-filled landscape, wondering what on earth had just happened to them. Answers, there were none. Not surprisingly, they quickly headed home, their galloping horses getting them there in a timely fashion.

It is rather intriguing to note that Evans-Wentz's source told him that in the days and weeks ahead he experienced repeated encounters with these strange entities that started out as flames within balls of light and that took on humanoid forms. Unfortunately, Evans-Wentz was not told the specifics of these additional experiences, only that they had occurred in both Ireland and England and all before the end of 1911, thus giving Evans-Wentz enough time to reference them in his classic book.

Selkies, Shapeshifters of the Sea

Within the history of fairy lore, there exists a longstanding tradition of these magical—and sometimes manipulative, dangerous, and even deadly—entities having the ability to shapeshift into a nearly dizzying number of forms. We'll begin with one of the lesser known creatures that falls into the fairy category. Its name is the selkie, a beast that is most associated with the people and the old folklore of northern Scotland, the Shetland and Orkney Islands, Ireland, and Iceland. It's fair to say that the selkie is not too dissimilar to the legendary mermaid, although, as will become apparent, there are significant differences, too.

Like the mermaid—and its male equivalent, the merman—the selkie is an animal that dwells deep in ocean waters and has a long-standing connection to the human race. Also like the mermaid, the selkie is said to be a seducer supreme. Whereas, in times past, mermaids and mermen were perceived as being half human and half fish in appearance, they were not shapeshifters per se. Rather, they were a combination of creatures. The selkie, however, has the unique ability to take on two specific forms: that of a seal and that of a human, both male and female. Whereas mermaids are limited to living in the oceans, the selkie exists as a seal in the water and as a human on land. It achieves the latter by discarding its seal skin and taking on human form—that of a beautiful, alluring woman or a handsome, muscular man.

While the selkie is certainly a manipulative creature—as all fairies are said to be—it is not a malicious one, at least not for the most part. Not only do selkies have a deep affinity for the human race, they are also attracted to us—physically, emotionally, and sexually. A selkie may live in the seas of our world for an extraordinarily long period of time. Should, however, one of these magical things develop a lusting for or an attraction to a human, they will cast off and carefully hide their sealskin and take to the land in human guise. A twist on this aspect of the legend maintains that if the human in question can locate the hidden hide, then the selkie will remain with that same person, and the selkie's love will last as long as their human companion lives.

Even when the selkie stays on the land with its lover, the time very often comes when the yearning to return to the sea becomes overpowering and, finally, irresistible. Generally speaking, the selkie—which, in typical fairy style, has an extremely long lifespan—will only do so when its human partner has passed on. When the grieving process is over, the selkie will then seek out the sealskin that it discarded and hid years earlier, take on its original seal form, and spend the rest of its life traveling the seas.

As for what the selkies really are, that is very much a matter of conjecture. Most people would likely relegate the entire matter to the world of folklore. Just maybe, however … most people might be wrong. One theory suggests that selkies are the souls of drowned seafarers, such as sailors and fishermen. The notion that the human dead can return to our plain of existence as animalistic shapeshifters is widespread. Then there is the theory that the selkies represent an ancient group of humans who, in the distant past, chose to return to the seas in which life began: they slowly took on new forms as they became more and more accustomed to living in the water.

A far more down-to-earth scenario concerns an ancient Hebrides clan, the MacCodrums. They were said to display one specific and unusual characteristic. It was a genetic anomaly that affected their hands, giving them a webbed and flipper-like appearance. And, as a direct result, it led to the creation of a rumor—one that eventually became perceived as hard fact—that the waters off the Scottish mainland were the collective domain of animals that were part human and part seal.

Whatever the truth of the matter, it is intriguing to note that despite having centuries-old origins, beliefs in the selkie still exist in certain parts of Scotland, its surrounding isles, and Iceland—which, today, is in stark contrast to the issue of mermaids; creatures which are almost universally seen as mythological entities. Indeed, David Thomson's 1954 book, *The People of the Sea*—which is a full-length study of the selkie saga—makes it abundantly clear that well into the twentieth century, the selkie was perceived by Scottish folk as a real, living shapeshifter.

Transforming into a Tree

Of the many and varied kinds of fairies that were said to possess the awesome powers of shapeshifting, certainly one of the most mysterious, and strangest of all, was the dryad. It was a definitive elemental of magical proportions that took shapeshifting to a truly unique level—as we shall now see. The dryad was a supernatural entity that features heavily in ancient Greek mythology and was exclusively associated with forests, woods, and trees. There was a very good reason for that: the dryad had the uncanny and eerie ability to transform itself into a tree!

In essence, the dryads were what, today, we would consider to be nature spirits—nymphs, one might be justified in saying. While within the teachings of ancient Greece the dryads were seen as the guardians and protectors of trees and of the woods, there was a related belief that they *were* the trees, that each and every tree had its own spirit, one that could appear in the form of the tree itself or as a sprite-like fairy being.

Different trees were possessed by—or could shapeshift into—different elementals and vice versa. For example, according to the Greeks, ash trees were the domain of the Meliai—most well-known within Greek mythology as the protectors and guardians of the mighty Greek god, Zeus, during his very earliest years. Mulberry bushes were cared for by a subgroup of dryads known as the Morea. The Syke did likewise for fig trees, as did the Balanos for the oak and Ptelea for the elm tree. There was a very good reason why so much care and dedication went into protecting the trees: should a tree die, then the elemental within it—or, depending on one's belief system, the entity that could shapeshift into the tree—would die, too. Just like the selkie of Scotland and Iceland, the dryads possessed the magical ability to transform themselves into beautiful women and handsome men, with the female entity being the most often reported.

Despite the ancient origins of the dryads, and just like the trees and forests around us, they have never really gone away. For example, they appear prominently in C. S. Lewis's hugely successful Chronicles of Narnia books and movies, demonstrating that despite the passage of time, the old traditions and beliefs still continue to prevail.

The Donas de Fuera

Finally, on the matter of fairies and shapeshifting, we have the *Donas de Fuera* of Sicily, which is an island in the Mediterranean Sea and a region of Italy. Very much like the elementals of England, Scotland, Ireland, and Wales, the Donas de Fuera were small, humanoid entities that had somewhat of a fraught relationship with the local, human population. Although there were both male and female beings, certainly it was the latter who were most visible when it came to interacting with the people of Sicily. While they were described as both beautiful and enchanting, the Donas de Fuera were not to be messed with. They certainly had their friendly and even helpful sides to their characters, but, if and when offended, their wrath ranged from cruel and dangerous to deadly.

The Donas de Fuera looked human—for the most part—aside from their strange feet, which were described as being circular or paw-like. The latter description is most apt, since the Donas de Fuera had the ability to turn themselves into cats—of the regular kind and also of a black variety of mountain-lion size. Reports of large, shapeshifting black cats can be found within the United Kingdom, too, interestingly.

13
ALIENS THAT PROBABLY AREN'T

IS IT POSSIBLE THAT some UFO encounters might not be what they initially appear to be—namely, face-to-face confrontations with extraterrestrials from faraway worlds? Might they actually be carefully stage-managed, manipulated events? Perhaps our presumed aliens are, in reality, shapeshifters from our world, entities that toy with our minds and assume the roles and even the appearances of ETs.

Today, when people ponder the matter of extraterrestrial encounters, they typically think of so-called alien abductions and the Grays, those diminutive, large-headed entities with eerie black eyes that are nearly hypnotic in nature. Back in the latter part of the 1940s and the early 1950s, however, things were very different. Infinitely different, even. Back then, the Grays were in the sights of precisely no one at all. That's not to say people weren't encountering aliens, however. They most assuredly were. Back then, however, they were known as the Space Brothers. They were very human-looking aliens—sometimes slightly shorter in stature than us and occasionally reaching heights of around seven feet. They wore long robes or silver outfits similar to the clothing worn by fighter pilots. And their message was always the same: they were deeply concerned by our growing nuclear arsenals and wished us to lay down our weapons and live in peace and harmony with one another—some chance of that happening anytime soon!

Among the more well known of all the contactees were George Adamski (whose 1952 book, *Flying Saucers Have Landed*, became a huge hit with not just UFO devotees but with the public, too), George Van Tassel (who attracted significant FBI attention as a result of his UFO claims), and Frank Stranges, who maintained that human-like ETs had infiltrated the Pentagon. And then there were the lesser-known contactees, one of whom is central to the story that this particular chapter is focused on. His name was Orfeo Angelucci. Although a fairly minor cog in the contactee wheel, Angelucci wrote a number of well-received books, even though they failed to sell in large quantities. They included *The Secret of the Saucers* and *Son of the Sun*. The nature of Angelucci's experiences will soon become very familiar to you.

According to the man himself—who was born in 1912 and worked for a New Jersey–based flooring company—it was in 1946 that his experiences of the other-world variety began, something which Angelucci reveals in *Son of the Sun*. Angelucci had a big interest in science and aviation and, in August 1946, launched a large balloon array into the skies of Trenton, New Jersey—the very town in which the aforementioned W. Y. Evans-Wentz was born in 1878. They were balloons filled with different kinds of mold—the reason being to determine if mold was affected by exposure to different altitudes, temperatures, and air pressure. Angelucci further maintained that it was this experiment that caught the attention of the Space Brothers, who specifically chose him to further their agenda on our planet.

Although Angelucci claimed numerous encounters with the cosmic brothers (and sisters, too), it was not so much the encounters themselves that were overly significant, but the means by which the entities from the stars manifested before him. It's important to note that although Angelucci stressed it was in the summer of 1946 that aliens first took note of his work with high-altitude balloons, it was not until 1952 that the cosmic ones met with him face to face. By this time, Angelucci had moved to California, specifically to Los Angeles. May 23, 1952, was the day—or, rather, the night—on which everything changed for Angelucci. It started out as a strange day even before the ETs arrived on the scene. From the moment he woke up, Angelucci felt agitated and worried and had a strange sense that the day was going to turn out very weird. He was right on target.

At the time, Angelucci was employed by the Lockheed Aircraft Corporation—which, interestingly enough, George Van Tassel had also been employed at, albeit in the 1940s—and was working a night shift. It was shortly after midnight on the evening in question that Angelucci got in his car and drove home. He didn't know it then, but he was about to have a detour and an experience of a very weird kind. It was as Angelucci crossed a bridge over the Los Angeles River—a bridge that was eerily empty of any other vehicles at the time—that he caught sight of a large, blue-colored ball of light that was clearly shadowing him. The beach ball–sized circle of light took a sudden turn, appearing directly in front of Angelucci's car. Shocked to the core, Angelucci slowed his car to practically walking pace and watched, amazed, as two small, green balls of light emerged from the larger one and floated toward him.

Via telepathy a booming voice informed Angelucci that he had indeed been watched ever since the day of that fateful balloon launch back in 1946. Angelucci was about to ask a question when the two balls closed in on each other, eventually merging into one larger green light. In mere seconds, the ball changed into the disembodied images of a man and a woman—or, as Angelucci came to learn, the floating heads of a pair of aliens who could pass for you or me. Like so many of the contactees, Angelucci was asked— in a noticeable and slightly bullying and patronizing fashion—to spread the word of the supposedly utterly benevolent ETs. "We'll be back," they said, when all was over, and in a slightly Arnold Schwarzenegger–fashion. The ball of light raced into the sky and Angelucci, a nervous character at the best of times, raced home.

The aliens were good to their word and arranged a following meeting—again late at night—under Los Angeles's Hyperion Avenue Freeway Bridge. As Angelucci patiently waited, he finally noticed a pair of small balls of green light approaching through the darkness. *They* were coming. The lights transformed into one single light, described by the man of the hour as something resembling a huge "soap bubble" that gave off a "pale glow." A chummy chat about the universe, destiny, life, death, and even the afterlife followed—although the chat was a strange one, given that Angelucci found himself speaking to a ball of light that spoke back to him. Then, suddenly, the light was gone, and Angelucci was left to do nothing stranger than head back home.

Three weeks later, and under cover of overwhelming darkness, Angelucci was back at the bridge—as were the two green lights. On this time, however, they shapeshifted into the forms of a man and a woman, whose appearance, said Angelucci, put them both at around the age of thirty-five. They referred to themselves as Orion and Lyra. Orion, the male entity, warned Angelucci that our solar system had been the home to numerous earlier civilizations that had destroyed themselves, and that unless we changed our dangerous ways, we would surely be next on the long and sorry list of casualties. It was for that very reason, Orion said, that Angelucci should write books on his experiences and get the word out to the public—which he duly and faithfully did, right up until his death in 1993, at the age of eighty-one.

Finally, it should be remembered that in the very similar 1910 experience related to W. Y. Evans-Wentz—involving two supernatural entities that manifested out of a pair of glowing balls of light—the source of the story had repeated, follow-up encounters. Just as Angelucci did. Indeed, when one compares the 1910 Ireland case—described by W. Y. Evans-Wentz in *The Fairy-Faith in Celtic Countries*—with Angelucci's experience in 1950s-era Los Angeles, one sees very little difference between the two. They practically mirror each other. That both Evans-Wentz and Angelucci were born in Trenton, New Jersey, makes the story even more bizarre.

"I Am Bosco"

In July 1952, a very similar encounter to those of Orfeo Angeucci was reported by a man named Karl Hunrath, who, at the time, lived in the city of Racine, Wisconsin. It is a story that is told in a 1953 declassified FBI file titled "Karl Hunrath." On the morning of July 22, Hunrath complained to his local police department about something very weird indeed, something that had occurred just a few hours earlier, in the dead of night. Who knows what the cops thought of it all, but it basically went as follows.

In the early hours of a Sunday morning in July, Hunrath's bedroom was flooded with a blinding, white light. He immediately sat upright and, as his eyes finally adjusted to the light, he could see in the corner of the room a floating ball of light that had a diameter of about four feet. Hunrath could only stare in shock and awe. Then, something amazing and terrifying happened: the glowing ball transformed into a well-dressed man in black, and Hunrath found himself temporarily paralyzed.

The "man" then proceeded to pump Hunrath's right arm full of chemicals—which rendered him into a distinctly altered state of mind—and proceeded to tell him that he had been chosen to play a significant role in the alien mission on Earth. A very groggy Hunrath could only look on from his bed as the somewhat foreign-sounding—but now perfectly human-appearing—alien told him, "I am Bosco. You have been chosen to enter our brotherhood of galaxies."

The suit-and-tie-wearing Bosco advised Hunrath that the brothers from beyond were deeply worried by our warlike ways, and so action had to be taken against those dastardly elements of the human race that wanted to spoil everyone else's fun. There was not to be any *The Day the Earth Stood Still*-style ultimatum for one and all, however. Nope. The aliens wished to recruit sympathetic humans to aid their righteous cause. Or, more correctly, get someone else to do all of their dirty work while they lurked safely in the shadows. And as Hunrath came to quickly realize, he was now one of the chosen few. But there was more. Bosco, via what Hunrath said were "occult techniques," uploaded into his mind countless amounts of data on how to build a terrible weapon that had the ability to destroy aircraft—specifically, the aircraft of the US military, whom the Space Brothers viewed as being just about as dangerous to world peace as the dastardly commies.

"I am Bosco, and that will be its name, too," boomed the alleged alien, in reference to the device that he wanted Hunrath to not just build, but also deploy. Far too stunned and drugged to move, Hunrath could only watch in a mixture of befuddlement and shock as Bosco then turned on his heels and left for his—one might be inclined to assume after an experience like that—flying saucer. There was no amazing "Beam me up, Scotty" exit for Bosco, however. For a ball of light that shapeshifted into a human-like extraterrestrial, Bosco had a very down-to-earth means of making good his departure: he pulled back the curtains of Hunrath's bedroom window, clambered out, and vanished into the depths of the early morning blackness of Hunrath's front yard!

The now-declassified FBI file reflects that Hunrath had assured the police there was no way he would even consider building Bosco and letting it loose on the world. Special agents of the Bureau were not quite so sure, however. The neighbors were soon complaining of strange noises coming from Hunrath's garage day and night, and at least three or four times per week he had a visitor who stayed for hours on end. Checks of the man's license plate by the FBI revealed he was a local: Wilbur J. Wilkinson—a subservient, Igor-like lackey to Hunrath's escalating Dr. Frankenstein. On a morning in early August, FBI agents made an unannounced visit to Hunrath's place of residence, demanding to be shown what it was that he and Wilkinson were working on in the garage. Weapon or not, to the FBI it appeared to be nothing more than "a collection of radios, and speakers and cables strung together." The somewhat bemused agents said their farewells and left. Had they been born into today's world, they might just as well have texted their boss, "Hunrath / Bosco: WTF?"

Whether or not Hunrath may have anticipated getting such a visit is unknown. But what we can be sure of is that Hunrath was now a man on a mission. And with the Bureau boys snooping around, Hunrath had no choice but to head for pastures new. There was only one way he was going to achieve his goal of fame and fortune and do the right thing by brother Bosco. It was time to say adios to both Wisconsin and the FBI and head to where all the alien action was then taking place: California. Hunrath and Wilkinson soon hooked up with the major players in West Coast Ufology at the time. They included such contactees as George Adamski and

George Hunt Williamson, as well as a number of UFO researchers and investigative groups. All was going well until November 1953. That was when things came to a mysterious and ominous end.

It was early on the morning of November 10 that Hunrath and Wilkinson rented a compact aircraft from a local airstrip. They headed off for what they claimed to several colleagues, just forty-eight hours earlier, was to be a face-to-face meeting with a group of extraterrestrials connected to Bosco. Although the pair was seen taking off from the airstrip headed in a direction that would have set them on a course for Palm Springs and Joshua Tree, they were never seen again. Despite extensive searches by the emergency services, Hunrath and Wilkinson were not found. No wreckage of the aircraft was ever found, either. Wilkinson's wife never heard from her husband again. They were gone. As in forever.

The strange story of Orfeo Angelucci and the Hunrath-Wilkinson affair could be considered just a couple of odd but engaging UFO encounters of the type that one rarely sees in today's world, except for one thing. Their experiences with the morphing balls of light parallel almost exactly what we saw occurred in early twentieth-century Ireland, as recorded by W. Y. Evans-Wentz. Yet, in that case, there was no extraterrestrial component, whatsoever—just fairy-like entities.

This begs a very important question: are the balls of light native to our world, rather than extraterrestrial? Probably, yes. That being so, perhaps their incredible ability to shapeshift allows them to toy with, manipulate, and tantalize the human race—for bizarre and obscure reasons that might be born out of a decidedly deranged sense of humor. Maybe, they enjoy passing themselves off as hair-covered hominids, as ETs, and as fairies—and amazing and terrifying us in the process—for one simple reason: *because they can.*

14
THE MOST DANGEROUS
SHAPESHIFTERS OF ALL

FROM THE MIDDLE EAST to Alaska and from Norway to Iceland, stories surface of shapeshifters that should be avoided at all costs. They are supernatural, cold-hearted entities that provoke overwhelming fear and dread—for reasons that will soon become very apparent.

The reverend Sabine Baring-Gould was someone who had a nearly lifelong interest in shapeshifters, and particularly so the traditional werewolf—or wolfman—of France, Germany, and Austria of the Middle Ages. As Baring-Gould dug further into the controversy of man becoming animal and man again, however, he developed a deep passion for the folklore and mythology of Iceland and Scandinavia—as well as for the many and varied mysterious creatures that dwelled in such countries. Baring-Gould's publication, *The Book of Werewolves*, reveals that of particular fascination to him were the *Eigi Einhamir*, which basically means "of more than one skin." There may not be a better way of describing a supernatural shapeshifter. The saga of the Eigi Einhamir dates far back into history—in fact, to the very earliest years of pagan times when Christianity had still yet to leave its mark on much of Europe.

Chiefly, the story of these enigmatic and dangerous people originates in Norway and Iceland. The Eigi Einhamir were a unique and mysterious band of mighty warriors who dwelled in the frozen wastelands and who could take on the form of just about any living entity that crossed their minds. The animals whose forms they assumed were referred to as the *Hamr*, while the actual process of bodily transformation was known as *Skipta Homum*. It wasn't just a case of physically mutating, however. Not only did the Eigi Einhamir take on the muscle power of the creature at issue, whether a bear, a wolf, or a wild cat, but their minds were majorly altered, too, to the point where the innate savagery and beastly natures of the animals overwhelmed both their human minds and thought processes.

The mutation did not occur as it did with the likes of the werewolf, however. On some occasions, the person's soul would leave their body and invade the mind of the animal, effectively taking it over. For the onlookers, it was a traumatic time, as—with the soul now in a new body—the original body lay rigidly and unmoving and seemingly in a state of death. At least, that is, until the soul returned to its original body. At that point, the person would then suddenly wake up, almost as if they were rising from the grave. *The Walking Dead*? Not quite, but not too far off either. Perhaps even more intriguing, the Eigi Einhamir had the nearly unique ability to take over the thought processes of people, plunging them into hypnotic-like, altered states and making it appear as if they had shapeshifted, when, on some occasions, it was all in the mind, so to speak.

There was one way, however, in which the Eigi Einhamir could be identified, regardless of the particular type of animal into which they morphed. It was by looking carefully at their eyes. That was the Eigi Einhamir's one and only weak spot: their eyes never changed from their original, human form. Even when the witness to their activities was in a hypnotized condition or when the soul of the Eigi Einhamir entered and took control of the animal's mind, the eyes of the beast were always the eyes of the shapeshifter. In that sense, identifying an animal that was not an animal—but one of the Eigi Einhamir, instead—was relatively easy. It would, after all, be very strange to see a wolf or a bear with eyes that were definitively human in appearance. When the eyes of a human were seen staring out of the face of a beast, those that feared the Eigi Einhamir took quick and decisive steps to end its malevolent and strange existence.

In the same way that silver bullets and fire are said to be the weak spots of werewolves everywhere, so were the eyes to the Eigi Einhamir.

Alaska's Deadly Resident Monster

The Wendigo is a very misunderstood monster, one that is a staple part of the folklore and legend of the Native American tribe known as the Algonquin. The monster is typically described as a tall, crazed, and violent thing that roams the forests of the Pacific Northwest, the northernmost states of the United States, and Canada. It is a large, humanoid beast that dines on human flesh. There is, however, another aspect to the lore surrounding the Wendigo. Namely, that if a person eats human flesh, he or she can shapeshift into a Wendigo. Adding to the legend, the Wendigo has the ability to take control of our minds—always for terrible and horrific reasons. In that sense, as well as a shapeshifting angle, there is what we might term a "mind-shifting" process, too.

Alaska, the domain of the Wendigo.

One of the more intriguing theories for what may have pro-voked the legends of the Wendigo is that they were based upon early, centuries-old reports of Bigfoot encounters. Certainly, there are more than a few reports in which Bigfoot-type beasts have acted violently in the presence of people. There are even reports of people vanishing in the woods and forests of the United States—amid theories that the Bigfoot, when food is scarce, will feed on just about anything. And that includes us.

And, as we will see in the section of this book on the Puerto Rican chupacabra, there is a handful of reports of chupacabra shapeshifting into a large, hair-covered beast of Bigfoot-style pro-portions—something that suggests that Bigfoot itself may have the ability to change its physical form. In that sense, it may not seem so far out, after all, to suggest the shapeshifting Wendigo and the North American Bigfoot are one and the same.

Of the various stories that surround the Wendigo, certainly the most horrific revolves around a Cree Native American named Swift Runner, who lived with his family in an area of forest close to Edmonton, Canada. It is a macabre tale told in Andrew Hanon's 2008 article "Evil Spirit Made Man Eat Family" and in Joey Storm Walker's "Swift Runner." As 1878 rolled over into 1879, Swift Runner turned up in the city of St. Albert, Canada. He told a bleak and harrowing story of how all of his family—his wife, his six children, his mother, and his brother—had fallen victim to the recent, hostile winter, in which food was beyond scarce and temperatures plunged. As plausible as the story told by Swift Runner to a group of Catholic priests sounded, there was a significant red flag. Swift Runner hardly looked emaciated. In fact, he looked very well fed. That's because he was: Swift Runner spent the winter devouring his entire family, eating their flesh and gnawing on their bones—as the St. Albert police found to their horror when they traveled to the site of his home in the woods.

Suspicions soon began to surface that Swift Runner was possessed by a Wendigo: he began to exhibit bizarre, animalistic activity, such as howling, growling, and screaming in savage fashion. Tales circulated that, on one occasion, Swift Runner was seen to transform into a savage-looking humanoid, a definitive Wendigo—something caused by his taste for human flesh.

Moving things into far more modern times, there is the eerie and creepy story of Timothy McLean—a man who was killed and eaten by his attacker. It all went down on the night of July 30, 2008, when McLean boarded a bus heading for Manitoba, Canada. McLean soon fell asleep, something that proved to be disastrous and deadly for McLean. As he slept, the passenger next to him, Vince Weiguang Li, violently stabbed McLean to death with a large knife. With others aboard the bus screaming for help, the driver brought the vehicle to a screeching halt and fled the bus. As they held the door shut from the outside to ensure that Li could not escape, the passengers looked on in horror as Li sliced McLean's head off and began to feast on the remains of his victim. The local police were quickly on the scene and Li was taken into custody. It was, however, all far too late for poor Timothy McLean.

There is a strange and unsettling footnote to all of this: only days before he savagely killed McLean, Li had been delivering in his local area copies of the *Edmonton Sun*, an edition that profiled the work of a man named Nathan Carlson, an expert on ... the Wendigo. It was a deeply strange situation, one that provoked rumors that Li, after reading the article, became possessed by a Wendigo. A disturbing thought, to say the least.

A Middle Eastern Shapeshifter

Of all the many and varied shapeshifters that populate our world, there is no doubt that the most feared and dreaded of all are the djinn. They are extremely dangerous and manipulative entities that can take on various forms and just as they see fit. It is ironic that the djinn, in reality, is such a feared and powerful creature. The irony stems from the fact that popular culture and the world of entertainment have collectively dumbed down the nature, power, and dark characters of the djinn. This is very much as a result of the production of the likes of the 1960s television show *I Dream of Jeannie* and the 1992 Disney movie *Aladdin*. There is, however, nothing amusing or lighthearted about the real djinn. They are the ultimate shapeshifting nightmares. And they will do all they can to get their claws into us—particularly so if we are reckless enough to invite or invoke them.

The djinn are entities that collectively amount to a significant part of ancient Islamic lore and teachings. Certainly, they feature prominently in the pages of the Qur'an. Muslim legend maintains that djinns are formed out of a form of smokeless fire. Djinn expert Rosemary Ellen Guiley has suggested that this may have been an ancient, early way of describing what, today, we would term plasma. Jesse Emspak, writing at LiveScience, says of plasma that it "is a state of matter that is often thought of as a subset of gases, but the two states behave very differently. Like gases, plasmas have no fixed shape or volume, and are less dense than solids or liquids. But unlike ordinary gases, plasmas are made up of atoms in which some or all of the electrons have been stripped away and positively charged nuclei, called ions, roam freely."

Rosemary Ellen Guiley, djinn authority.

The djinn are said to be life forms that came into being long before the human race was anywhere near on the horizon. In terms of their standing—as well as their supernatural nature—in ancient religious teachings, the djinn are on a par with the angels. Again according to the old texts, after Allah brought Adam into being, each and every angel was ordered to kneel before him. While they did exactly as they were ordered, the djinn did not. They were the ultimate rebels. The djinn overlord, Iblis, went against Allah—as did the rest of the djinns. The result, for them, was catastrophic: they were unceremoniously ejected from heaven, but they were given the right to rectify things when Judgment Day comes calling on us all—at least, according to the ancient stories.

Of course, the story of Iblis, his rebellious followers, and their ejection from a heavenly realm closely parallels the Holy Bible's story of the devil, deadly demons, and their very own hellish domain. Might demons and djinn be one and the very same but given somewhat different descriptions and histories according to the teachings of various religions? Yes, very possibly.

The aforementioned Rosemary Ellen Guiley suspects that the djinn exist in what we might call another dimension, a realm which is as unseen to us as it is impenetrable to us. But, for the djinn, negotiating multiple dimensions is second nature—which is specifically why they spend so much time causing havoc and horror in our reality.

Unlike us, the djinn have lifespans of such an incredible length that, compared to our measly eighty or ninety years, are akin to being almost immortal. They do, however, eventually die. In somewhat baffling fashion, given that they are said to be made out of plasma, djinns have the ability to reproduce; they have families and hierarchies and are of both sexes. They have homes, too. Their homes are far removed from ours, however.

The typical djinn traditionally prefers Middle Eastern hot deserts, caverns, ancient and ruined buildings, shadowy valleys, and deep tunnels. They are not particularly enamored by daylight, much preferring instead to rest when the sun is at its height and to surface when the landscape is dark and filled with shadows. This, in all likelihood, explains why so many people who report djinn encounters state that the experiences occurred after sunset and in the early hours of the morning, and specifically and usually between 1:30 a.m. and 3:00 a.m.—which parallels the malevolent activities of incubus and succubus. Djinn are also said to be great lovers of music of all kinds, but particularly that played on a sitar.

Exactly how many djinn exist—or have ever existed—is unknown; however, their extensive lifespans, combined with their abilities to procreate, suggests that they are many in number. Perhaps even millions, which is an extremely disturbing thought. This provokes an important question: If djinn are regularly entering our world from their own dimension, then why do we not see them? According to the old tales, there is a very good answer to that question: the djinn are invisible to the human eye. Interestingly, however, those same old tales maintain that both donkeys and dogs have the ability to see djinn and are able to pick up on their nature, which can range from good to dangerous. In that sense, if you have a pet dog that regularly stares intently at one particular part of your living room and he or she reacts by shaking and whimpering, then you may have a djinn in your very midst. Not a pleasing thought, not in the slightest. In a somewhat paradoxical state, however, the djinn are said to keep dogs as pets—in much the same way that we do.

So, why, precisely, are the djinn so tied to us, the human race? Rosemary Ellen Guiley offers the following, which is undeniably worrying: "They can eat human food when they take human form, but our food does not sustain them. It gives them pleasure. They can absorb the essence of food, and things like the molecules from tobacco smoke, which provide enjoyment. Their main source of nourishment is the absorption of energy from life forms. The best is the draining of a soul, but is difficult to do and is considered unlawful. It is, however, practiced by certain powerful renegade djinn. The vampiric absorption of the life force can be quite detrimental to people, and cause health problems."

There you have it: for the djinn we are a source of food. But that is not all. The djinn clearly enjoy taunting and tormenting us, too. Sometimes, this can be to a mild degree, and even relatively innocuous in nature, with djinn moving items in the home of their target and placing them in other rooms. This is an issue that mirrors the odd antics of so-called Tricksters like elementals, who enjoy manipulating us—chiefly for their own warped amusement. More often than not, however, the djinn display highly dangerous activity. That very often begins with disrupting electrical equipment—everything from microwaves to refrigerators, computers to telephones, and electric lights to ovens.

Sometimes a djinn will perform a favor for its target—which is specifically where the concept of the "genie" and the "three wishes" derived its origins. But, it is almost always a favor that backfires, leaving the person in a far worse state than before the djinn ever manifested. Far more disturbing: the djinn can cause a person to fall sick—and typically dangerously so—and even to die. Paranormal infection is very often the name of their grim game.

Perhaps most malevolent of all is the ability of the djinn to possess the mind of a person. Again, we see a parallel with biblical teachings, namely matters relative to the issue of demonic possession. This matter of the djinn effectively taking control of, and enslaving, the mind of a specific person most often occurs when that very same person summons up a djinn. What this demonstrates is that not only can we call forth djinn—providing, of course, that we know the correct ancient rites that are required to do so—but that when we do so, we can then become their very next victim.

As for the shapeshifting qualities of the djinn, they are as many as they are varied. Rather notably, our old friend, the glowing-eyed Phantom Black Dog, is one of the most favored forms a djinn will appear as, particularly so when it wishes to operate in our world, as is a snake. Indeed, according to Islamic lore, if a snake enters one's home, it may not be a normal, regular snake. In all likelihood, the old lore states, it is a shapeshifted djinn.

Rosemary Ellen Guiley believes, and states in her book *The Vengeful Djinn*, that the djinn manifest in numerous other forms, too. The long list includes aliens, the spirits of once-living people, fairies, creatures that fall into the cryptozoological domain, and even angels. So clever, manipulative, and cunning is the djinn that it is incredibly difficult to determine which of the above is real and which is nothing more than a djinn in disguise.

15
LYCANTHROPY:
A STRANGE STATE OF MIND

THE HUMAN MIND IS capable of many things, including creating the illusion that a person has taken on animal form. For all intents and purposes, anyone seeing a person affected in such a fashion would not notice any physical changes, although they would certainly note their savage behavior. For the victims, however, they are absolutely convinced they are no longer human, but something more, something animal-like and monstrous.

Clinical lycanthropy is a strange, and not entirely understood, phenomenon that makes a person believe they have the ability to change into wild animals—whether by choice or as a result of circumstances wholly out of their control. While lycanthropes report mutating into all manner of animals, including tigers, jaguars, eagles, foxes, hyenas, and cats, there's no doubt that the dominating animal when it comes to this curious medical condition is the wolf—which is precisely why the image of the werewolf, as a person becoming a monster, proliferates to such a degree.

It's important to note that clinical lycanthropy and lycanthropy are not one and the same. The former is a delusion that one becomes a monster, while lycanthropy is, allegedly at least, a literal, physical change. Those with clinical lycanthropy exhibit extraordinary traits, including crawling around on all fours, growling, howling, and even attacking people. Suggestions have been made that it is linked to such conditions as schizophrenia, although that is very much an issue of debate and controversy. All that can be said with 100 percent certainty is that for the affected person the experience is all too real—even if it is generated by the complexities of the human mind.

There's very little doubt that at least some cases of clinical lycanthropy prompted a number of reports of werewolves in centuries long gone—and which led the affected people to murder and mutilate on a large and horrific scale, particularly so in Europe of the Middle Ages. As we shall now see.

Peter Stubbe, an Insane Monster

A perfect example of how lycanthropy can radically affect the mind of a person—never mind those who cross the paths with lycanthropes—is the deeply disturbing saga of a man named Peter Stubbe. It is a story told in "Trials: The Damnable Life and Death of Peter Stubbe, 1589–90" at the blog *Werewolf Theory*, and a transcript of the contemporary record of the affair by George Bores is reproduced online through the University of Michigan.

It was in the latter part of the sixteenth century that Stubbe went on a veritable rampage of mutilation, cannibalism, and murder in and around the German towns of Bedbur and Cperadt. The story, however, goes back to Stubbe's childhood. At the age of just eleven, Stubbe's grandmother—who had a reputation as someone who was deeply learned in what are generally known as the black arts—introduced him to a world that most people never get to see. Or even *want* to see.

While Stubbe was an absolute textbook case of clinical lycanthropy, there's very little doubt that his crone-like grandmother certainly helped worsen his deranged state of mind—although whether she did so deliberately or out of ignorance we'll likely never know for sure. For around a decade, young Stubbe was exposed to the worlds of sorcery, necromancy, sacrificial rites, and altered states of mind. What were described as "infernal fiends" were conjured up from wretched realms by Stubbe, who finally gave himself—body, mind, and soul—to none other than Satan himself. Of course, such Faustian pacts rarely, if ever, work out in a positive fashion for the person trying to do a deal with the head honcho of hell. And, certainly, Stubbe's case was no different.

It was when Stubbe found himself in the grip of Satan—or in the throes of mental illness, or both—that local mayhem in the vicinity of Cperadt and Bedbur erupted in terrifying, murderous fashion. So the story went, Satan thundered to Stubbe that whatever he desired, he could have. Money, women, or power—the list went on and on. Stubbe replied that he didn't want any of those things. All he wanted was to kill, to maim, and to devour. His targets: people.

It's hardly surprising that Satan was more than happy with the warped mindset of his latest lackey. In 1590, George Bores translated a study of Stubbe and his ways, commonly known as "The Damnable Life and Death of Stubbe Peeter." The study recounted that Satan saw Stubbe as "a fit instrument to perform mischief as a wicked fiend pleased with the desire of wrong and destruction." The story involved another instrument, too. Namely, a supernatural girdle that Satan ordered Stubbe to tie around his waist—which he did, eager to please the master of the underworld. In no time at all, Stubbe began to change—and not in a good way. At least, not from our perspective and definitely not for his unfortunate victims.

No sooner had Stubbe placed the girdle around his middle that he suddenly started to change—in both body and mind, so the legend goes, anyway. His body grew a thick coat of fur. His hands turned into huge paws equipped with sharp, lethal talons. His face changed to the point where his jaw took on the form of a wolf-like muzzle. His mouth grew wide and his teeth became definitive fangs. As for his psychological state, Stubbe's mind became less than that of a man and far more than that of an animal, one driven by nothing more than basic instinct and a savage urge to slaughter. And slaughter he did, to a huge degree.

No one—young or old—was safe in the Cperadt-Bedbur area. As Stubbe entered his twenties, numerous reports surfaced of bodies found in the surrounding forests and fields—all with their throats savagely torn out, many disemboweled, and most missing significant amounts of blood. For a while, the identity of the killer remained unknown. As for Stubbe, he was under absolutely no one's suspicion. Indeed, in his human form, Stubbe would brazenly stroll through the local hamlets, bidding people good day, tipping his hat, and playing with the local children. Little did the townsfolk know it, but many of those same people were to become Stubbe's victims in the days, weeks, and months ahead. Even *years*. Men he slaughtered. Children he devoured. And women he raped and then killed. Unfortunately for his targets, they had little chance of escaping his clutches. Or of escaping death, either. His wolfish state allowed him to run at incredible speeds, effectively ensuring that no one could outpace him. Indeed, Stubbe's actions were likened to those of a sheepdog herding sheep in the field. The big difference, however, was that Stubbe had murder on his mind—

constantly. It was a sinister state of affairs that lasted for around a quarter of a century.

Like most deranged serial killers, however, Stubbe finally made a series of mistakes during the course of his killings, something that led him to being identified as the crazed murderer that he was, like being seen when he removed the girdle and immediately returned to his far less fearsome-looking regular form of Peter Stubbe. The local constabulary quickly brought swift justice to the table. He was given two choices: confess to everything immediately or suffer severe torture until he finally caved in. Like so many serial killers, Stubbe could dish out death and mayhem, but he was far from good at receiving it. He coughed up immediately, hoping for mercy. No chance of that. Mercy, there was none. As an example of his character, Stubbe gave up both his daughter and one Katherine Trompkin as conspirators in helping him to hide his tracks.

The result was grim: Stubbe's daughter and Trompkin were tied to stakes and burned alive. Stubbe was strapped to a large, wooden wheel, and large metal pincers were used to tear the skin off his bones. A wooden hammer was used to break both his legs and his arms. And, for good measure, he was decapitated and his body turned to smoldering ashes.

For the people of the area, there was no doubt that Peter Stubbe was someone who, while in league with Satan, achieved the ability to transform himself into a werewolf, and commit murder on a shocking, decades-long scale. Today, we might justifiably say that it was literally a case of being all in the mind. Certainly, clinical lycanthropy is a recognized psychological condition—one that requires treatment at the earliest opportunity possible. Cases similar to that of Peter Stubbe proliferate. For our purposes, one more will suffice.

It revolves around a Frenchman, a tailor whose name has become lost to the fog of time but who became known as the Werewolf of Châlons. He had been seen changing from man to wolf and embarking on terrible rampages. A Parisian, he killed and devoured a number of young children, and, as a result, in 1598 he was burned alive for his crimes.

It should be noted that there is one issue that has never been satisfactorily answered for those that have studied the phenomenon: If it is nothing more than mental illness, why do so many of the sufferers believe they turn into a wolf? Yes, there are examples of people claiming to have morphed into the forms of cats, bats, and foxes, but the wolf remains a dominating form. It's a question to ponder as we take a look at the next part of our story, one that takes us into the domain of conspiracy, the CIA, and government-orchestrated mind-control operations.

Mind Monsters on the Loose in France

Many might find the idea of shapeshifting being connected to the worlds of secret agents, bizarre and top-secret experiments, and the manipulation of the mind to be way too extreme to accept. But, they would be wrong. Sometimes, truth really is stranger than fiction—and in ways that are scarcely imaginable. The story in question dates back to a hot summer's day in the early 1950s and a little French town called Pont-Saint-Esprit, which is located in the southern part of the country. The town is a tranquil one, filled with a great deal of history dating back to the 1700s. Today, however, it is a decidedly infamous locale—chiefly as a result of a series of events that began on August 15, 1951. That was the date upon which all hell broke loose around Pont-Saint-Esprit, and numerous townsfolk took on the guises of marauding animals—in their minds, at least.

The official story is that the people of the town were the victims of a certain fungus called ergot, which can affect rye. It does far more to the person who eats the infected rye: it provokes graphic and terrifying hallucinations, as werewolf and shapeshifter authority Linda Godfrey makes clear. She says in her 2006 book, *Hunting the American Werewolf*, that "ergot is now widely regarded as a possible cause of the bestial madness. According to this theory, it was not demonic influence but the ingestion of *Claviceps purpurea* (which contains a compound similar to LSD), which led to the demented behavior and thus, executions, of many alleged witches, werewolves, and vampires."

The day began as a normal one for the people of this laid-back, picturesque old town. By sundown, however, it was like a scene out of *The Walking Dead*: what seemed to amount to raging infection was everywhere, and those free of that same perceived infection cowered behind locked doors, fearful of becoming the next victims of whatever it was that had cursed Pont-Saint-Esprit. Hundreds of people rampaged around town in bestial states, growling, howling, and causing havoc and mayhem. Others swore they saw their fellow townsfolk change into hideous creatures, such as werewolves, gargoyles, and demons. All told, close to 260 people were affected. Seven died. And more than four dozen were so psychologically traumatized that they were temporarily held at local asylums—for the good of themselves and for the unaffected people of the town, too.

But was ergot really the cause of the devastation and death? Here's where things become really controversial. One of those who have dug deep into the mystery of what erupted on August 15, 1951, is H. P. Albarelli Jr. He is the author of a huge book titled *A Terrible Mistake*. It's an immense 826-page-long investigation of the mysterious 1951 death of a man named Frank Olson, a brilliant chemist who, in the early 1950s, worked for the US Army's Special Operations Division at Camp Detrick. Today, it is called Fort Detrick and is where the military undertakes research and studies into such issues as chemical warfare, biological warfare, and deadly viruses.

Back in the early 1950s, however, the matters of so-called mind-control and Manchurian candidates were very much staple parts of Camp Detrick's work. But, for Olson, who was at the forefront of the mind-altering technology, his work was not destined to last. Nor was his life. Olson died on November 28, 1953, as a result of an, *ahem*, "fall" from the tenth floor of the Statler Hotel in Manhattan. Today, the overriding theory is that Olson—who began to regret working on the controversial programs—was forcibly thrown out of the window of the room by agents who were fearful Olson was about to blow the lid on the sheer extent to which unwitting people had been dosed with psychedelics, chemical concoctions, and various other mind-manipulating substances, all in the name of national security. But what does any of this have to do with shapeshifters? Let's see.

It's a fact that Frank Olson—while liaising with French intelligence counterparts—traveled to France in both 1950 and 1951, the latter being the year in which the town of Pont-Saint-Esprit became a bedlam, as Albarelli notes. The French were as interested as the Americans (and the Russians and the Brits, too, as it transpired) in how the human mind could be clandestinely manipulated. In view of all this, it's very notable that Olson's name turns up in previously highly classified CIA documents on the events at Pont-Saint-Esprit. One such document, which has surfaced through the terms of the US Freedom of Information Act—the title of which is blacked-out for national security reasons—states, "Re: Pont-Saint-Esprit and F. Olson files. SO Span/France Operation file, including

Olson. Intel files. Hand carry to Berlin—tell him to see to it that these are buried."

While this communication is couched in cagey and careful language, it clearly links Olson to Pont-Saint-Esprit, and it abundantly demonstrates that whatever really happened—and what led to people believing they and their friends were changing into wild beasts—had to be kept hidden at all costs. "Buried," even. Maybe one of those costs was Frank Olson's life. Albarelli makes it clear that, in his opinion, the town of Pont-Saint-Esprit was deliberately targeted by powerful and shadowy figures who wanted to know the extent to which the human mind could be messed around with on a large scale—and they chose August 15, 1951, as the date to initiate the experiment. Theories include a powerful psychedelic inserted into the town's water supply, a more than liberal amount of LSD utilized in similar fashion, and possibly even an airborne aerosol sprayed over the town, crop-dusting style.

Whatever the answer, the good folk of Pont-Saint-Esprit have not forgotten that terrible day when the people of the town became monsters—in their minds, if not physically.

16
MEN IN BLACK
AND BLACK-EYED CHILDREN

THE DOMAIN OF THE supernatural is filled to the brim with a wide and varied body of shapeshifters. A relatively new addition to the creepy club is the Black-Eyed Children phenomenon, which has far more than a passing connection to the notorious Men in Black of UFO lore. So far as can be determined, the BEC puzzle kicked off in the late 1990s. And, as will soon be revealed, these particularly eerie kids, like so many other strange beasts, have the ability to manipulate their physical forms.

Before we get to the cases, it's important to understand why the Black-Eyed Children were given the name that has since become so notorious in paranormal circles. Most witnesses to these strange children describe them as being aged between ten and fourteen. They are usually noticeably skinny, and they have very pale skin—to the point of looking deathly ill, even if they're actually not. They generally dress in black hoodies, which are usually pulled down to ensure that very little of their faces can be seen. There is a very good reason for this: the eyes of the BEC are solid black.

Their modus operandi is very much like that of their adult counterparts, the aforementioned Men in Black. They almost always surface late at night, knocking on doors and ringing doorbells, and with one single goal in mind: namely, to find a way into the targeted person's home. Sometimes, they claim to be lost and ask if they can come in and use the phone to call their parents. On other occasions, they say they are homeless—can they have some food and drink? Of course, when the targeted person catches sight of those black, soulless eyes, they quite understandably slam the door shut—as all of us surely would! So, we don't really know why, exactly, they have such a pressing desire to invade people's homes—but, nevertheless, that does appear to be their disturbing agenda.

The Phenomenon Kicks Off

So far as can be determined, the phenomenon of the Black-Eyed Children began in 1998—specifically in Abilene, Texas. It was late one night that a local news reporter named Brian Bethel had a run-in with a pair of such strange children. Darkness had fallen when Bethel reached a local mall, with the intention of dropping off a check in a secure mailbox. As he wrote the check, Bethel was jolted by a knock on the window of his car. Two, pale-skinned kids stood before him, one of which asked if they could get a ride home, specifically to get some money so that they could go to the local cinema. For Bethel, however, there was something very wrong about the pair. He couldn't put his finger on it, but there was something just not right about the odd, almost staged situation. An uneasy atmosphere enveloped Bethel—and became terror-filled when he caught sight of the eyes of both boys. At this stage, I surely don't need to tell you what color they were. Both amazed and scared witless, Bethel exited the area at high speed, leaving the

BECs far behind. A definitive mystery was born, one that shows no signs of going away anytime soon.

David Weatherly, the leading researcher
of the black-eyed children mystery.

The undeniable expert in this field is David Weatherly, whose 2012 book, *The Black Eyed Children*, is packed with case upon case of reports of the weirdest kids of all. Weatherly also addresses the various theories that have been put forward to try and explain the mystery. Those theories include ravenous ghosts, alien-human hybrids, demons, phantoms, and our old friends, the incubus and the succubus. This latter theory is notable for one particular fact: the Black-Eyed Children have the ability to shapeshift.

Granted, this aspect of the BEC phenomenon is not a widespread one, but the fact that it has been reported on more than a couple of occasions ensures that it warrants a place in the pages of this book.

A Late-Night Encounter

"Anna" is a twenty-nine-year-old resident of none other than Point Pleasant, West Virginia—the infamous locale where, in 1966, the notorious, blazing-eyed Mothman first surfaced, and which was made legendary in John Keel's classic book *The Mothman Prophecies*. As Anna revealed to me when I was at Point Pleasant in 2014 to speak at the annual Mothman Festival, back in October 2012 she had a strange and frightening encounter with a pair of Black-Eyed Children, late one Saturday night. Anna, a shift worker at a local factory, was spending her night relaxing and watching television, after a hard day of work. Sometime around 11:10 p.m., there was a knock at the door. Do I need to tell you who had just arrived?

Anna warily went to the door, and peered through the spyhole. She couldn't fail to see the two boys, standing next to each other, and both wearing the familiar black hoodies. She shouted through the door, asking what they wanted. When she got no answer, Anna put the chain on the door and opened it. When Anna saw the boys, she was frozen with terror: both had the ubiquitous black eyes, and both had skin the color of milk. "We need food," said one, in an almost robotic fashion, while looking at his feet. Oddly, his companion was also steadfastly looking down. In hindsight, Anna felt that their stances reflected their attempts to try to prevent her from seeing their strange eyes. If so, it was an attempt that failed spectacularly.

Anna slammed the door, shaking with fear as she did so. For a few minutes she retreated to the farthest part of the living room. When, however, there was no further knock at the door, she made a tentative move. Plucking up all her courage, Anna peered once again through the spyhole: the two boys were still there. Most disturbing of all, although Anna practically tiptoed toward the door and did not touch it as she reached it, she said that the BECs clearly reacted as she looked at them, as if they were able to sense she was just behind the other side of the door.

As Anna continued to stare at them—locked into a state of terror—something almost unimaginable happened: an eerie green glow surrounded the boys and, in seconds, they were replaced by a pair of what Anna described as large, upright lizards. The monstrous pair stood around eight feet tall, were completely naked, and had long, protruding jaws filled with razor-sharp teeth. They did nothing but stand there, for around twenty seconds or so, after which, Anna explained, the outside porch was enveloped in blackness and they vanished from view. Her first thought was to call the local police. But, she felt—almost certainly correctly—that filing such an incident with law enforcement officials would very likely cause her even more problems. Instead, she quickly packed a bag, carefully opened the door, raced to her car, and spent the next three days staying at her mother's place, just over the Ohio River. It was the end of a shocking and unforgettable incident.

Morphing Men in Black

Make mention of the notorious MIB and most people will instantly think of Will Smith and Tommy Lee Jones—such is the incredible success of the *Men in Black* movie franchise, which began back in the 1990s. Of course, those with an interest in the paranormal mysteries of our world will know that the movies were based upon real reports of encounters with mysterious, dangerous men dressed in black, ones who were intent on silencing people who had encountered UFOs, aliens, and even the likes of Bigfoot and the Mothman. There is, however, one big difference between Hollywood's MIB and those of the real world. Smith and Jones's characters—J and K—are the employees of a secret agency that oversees the alien presence on our planet. In other words, they are what we might accurately term Ufological 007s. In reality, however, the Men in Black are clearly not government agents: they don't even look human. In all probability, that's because they're not.

Just like the Black-Eyed Children, the Men in Black are often reported as having pale skin, a completely emotion-free demeanor, and a pressing need to enter the homes of the people they unsettlingly fixate upon. Unfortunately for the witnesses to paranormal phenomena, the MIB are usually extremely successful at gaining entry—which is at extreme odds with what we hear in Black-Eyed Children–based cases. There is one other similarity between the MIB and the BEC: their ability to shapeshift.

Albert Bender, who died in 2016 at the age of ninety-four, was a resident of Bridgeport, Connecticut, and someone whose encounters with the MIB in the early 1950s led to the subject being taken seriously and also ensuring that it became a staple part of Ufology. Bender, in 1951, established the International Flying Saucer Bureau, a group with ties to similar UFO-themed research groups all across the planet. In 1953, however, everything came crashing down on Bender: he was visited by three Men in Black who warned him to quit Ufology—as Bender graphically described in his 1962 book, *Flying Saucers and the Three Men*. Either that or die. It wasn't much of a choice for poor, terrified Bender. He did as he was told. As the Men in Black surely knew he would.

Unlike the movie versions, Bender's MIB did not knock loudly on the door and demand to be let in. Rather, they materialized in his bedroom, amid an overpowering smell of brimstone, in shadowy and ethereal form. And they had piercing, shining eyes, too. Locals they definitely were not. In seconds, the shadowy, almost gaseous, MIB took on physical forms and the threats were piled on big time. Bender got the message and quickly quit Ufology—albeit only to very briefly return in 1962 to write *Flying Saucers and the Three Men*. Afteward, Bender and UFOs parted company, never again to cross paths. Bender was not, however, the only person to claim that the MIB were able to change their form.

An Old Man Comes Calling

"Pauline," whom I interviewed in 2013, had a very strange encounter with a Man in Black back in October 1973, when she was living in Pasadena, California. It's notable, and probably relevant, for me to reveal that a major UFO wave was going on at that time, and all across the United States. While hiking in the California hills one Sunday morning, Pauline encountered a classic, silver-colored, flying saucer–style UFO that was high in the sky. Suddenly, it dropped to around fifty or sixty feet above her, hanging there in an odd, wobbling fashion. Amazed, Pauline could only stare as the silent craft bobbed around—like a boat on churning waters—and then shot away at high speed.

Pauline raced home and excitedly told her family of what had just taken place. They, apparently, weren't the only ones who knew what had occurred on the fateful morning in 1973. Three days later, after sunset, Pauline had a visitor. Not a welcome one, I should stress. It was a Man in Black, a skinny—almost emaciated—old man dressed in a shabby black suit, looking pale and ill and wearing an old, 1950s-style fedora hat.

Pauline said that she felt her mind was briefly enslaved, as the MIB nearly hypnotically asked her to invite him into her home. In a slight daze, and to her eternal cost, she did exactly that. She retreated to the couch, stumbling slightly and feeling ice cold. The old man followed her and stood in the living room, looming over her as he warned her—in no uncertain terms—never to discuss her close encounter again. Ever. The MIB then turned around and headed to the door. At that exact same moment, Pauline felt her mental faculties return to normal, and she raced after him, just as he exited the door and closed it behind him. Pauline threw the door open wide, only to find the old Man in Black gone. In his place, however, was something else: it was a large, black dog with bright red eyes. It snapped and snarled in Pauline's direction in what was clearly a deeply malevolent, dangerous fashion.

She stared in horror as the glowing-eyed monster prowled around the yard, clearly intent on adding to the malevolent atmosphere that was already firmly in place. Suddenly, as if out of nowhere, a large, black Cadillac—that looked decades-old in design—appeared and screeched to a halt outside of Pauline's home. It should be noted here that the MIB almost always drive such cars of that particular type, age, and color.

Pauline watched, shocked and scared, as the back door on the driver's side opened and the fiendish black hound bounded across the front yard and leapt into the back of the Cadillac, which shot away at high speed!

Today, Pauline—now a grandmother and someone who is fairly comfortable about sharing her bizarre experience—is of a firm opinion that the aged MIB and the red-eyed beast were one and the same. As Pauline sees it, it was something unexplainable but also something that could take on "different disguises" as it saw fit. As controversial as that might sound, let's not forget that we saw in a previous chapter how, in England of centuries ago, so-called Phantom Black Dogs were said to possess the ability to shapeshift into human form and vice versa.

The MIB over the Road

Moving on but still focused on Pasadena, California—interestingly enough—there is the very strange story of the "Maxwell" family, whom I met and spoke with in 2014. In the summer of 1987, they spent a week vacationing in and around San Francisco, staying with friends in Menlo Park. On their way back home, they traveled along California's famous Highway 101, which provides a panoramic view of the Pacific Ocean for mile upon mile. They chose to drive through the night, when the highway would be at its least busy, thinking that it would be to their benefit. How completely and utterly wrong they were. As fate would destine to have it, after a couple of hours of driving, the family of four spotted a strange light in the sky. It was described as a bright green ball of light about the size of a beach ball, and it paced their car and that stayed with them for a couple of miles at a height of around sixty feet. There was nothing frightening about the encounter. Rather, they were all amazed and excited. It wasn't long, however, before things got very disturbing.

The day after the Maxwells got home was a Sunday, meaning they had an extra day before returning to work and school. It was while one of the teenaged children was sitting on the porch and playing music on an old Walkman that she caught sight of a man on the other side of the road. He was dressed completely in black, aside from a white shirt. He even wore black gloves, on what was a bright, summery day. The girl was particularly disturbed by the fact that the man sported a weird grin and was staring right at her. So unsettled was she that she went back into the home and told her father of what had just happened. He quickly went to the door but—no surprise—the MIB was gone.

Later that same night, the girl had a frightening and graphic dream—if that is all it was—of the very same Man in Black standing next to her bed and staring at her in malevolent style. She woke suddenly, around 3:00 a.m., soaked in sweat. On the following night, the girl's younger brother had a similar dream. And, two days later the husband and wife saw a pair of creepy, pale MIB clearly watching, and following, them in a local supermarket. Oddly, as the husband, angry and confused by what was going on, decided to confront them, they headed quickly to another aisle and vanished—literally. They were nowhere to be seen.

Matters reached their conclusion on the next night, when Mr. Maxwell was woken up by the sounds of loud scratching at the front door—scratching that strongly suggested some form of wild animal was trying to get in the home, which is reminiscent, of course, of the strange saga of the Defiance, Ohio, werewolf of 1972. He decided to try to catch the beast off guard and raced into the backyard and to a gate that gave access to a small alley between his house and the house next door. He crept along, reached the front of the house, and peered at the front door. To his horror, there was no monster, but a man—in black, it scarcely needs saying—crouched down and pawing at the door in a deranged style.

Mr. Maxwell shouted in his direction, at which point the MIB stopped what it was doing, stood up to a height of around seven feet, and stared directly at him. Then, in an instant, the figure dropped to the floor, took on a wolf-like appearance, and bounded off into the darkness, leaving a shell-shocked and trauma-filled witness behind it. The MIB that became a wolf was not seen again, and the Maxwells did not experience anything else untoward. The strange series of events was finally at its end.

17
THE NATIVE AMERICAN CONNECTION

COYOTE IS ONE OF the most mysterious and magical creatures within the mythology of Native Americans and is noted for its shapeshifting abilities. Before we get to that issue, however, a bit of background information on the animal is first required. Coyotes are of the dog family and are formidable and deadly hunters. While they typically go for small prey, like rabbits and squirrels, they have been known to take on fully grown deer and even cattle. They are noted for their swimming skills and for the fact that they can run at the astonishing speed of almost forty miles per hour. That all said, there is another side to the coyote, one that revolves around shapeshifting.

Perceived almost unanimously by Native Americans as a trickster, Coyote is said to have the ability to control the weather, specifically rain and storms. And, like so many other trickster entities—such as fairies and goblins—he can be friendly, playful, and helpful. But, and also like all tricksters, Coyote has a dark side: it can be manipulative, deceitful, and even deadly, as the mood takes it. As for what Native American lore says of the shapeshifting abilities of Coyote, we are told that the animal can take on human form—usually in the guise of a man with a large mustache. Coyote is said to be able to transform into the forms of birds, fish, and cats. Also according to Native American mythology, witches and those familiar with magical rituals can transform themselves into coyotes. Thus, a coyote seen running wildly late at night may well be a shapeshifting witch or wizard, embarking on some dark and disturbing mission.

And we are far from being done with Coyote and its skills as a shapeshifter. There is a longstanding tradition among Native Americans that Coyote will stalk hunters in the woods and on the plains. Then, when it closes in on its victim, Coyote will supernaturally shed its coat, which it quickly throws over its quarry. It is this action that allows Coyote to shapeshift into the exact appearance of its victim. Typically, legend suggests, this is done to allow the animal to have sex with the wife of the victim—Coyote, in folklore, having a particular liking for women.

While many people might relegate such accounts to the domain of legend, the matter of shapeshifting and coyotes continues in the world of today. It is an issue that brings us back to the mystery of the chupacabra.

It was in 1995 that the phenomenon of the chupacabra exploded across the island of Puerto Rico. In the early 2000s, however, reports began to surface suggesting that the chupacabra had somehow made its way to the United States—specifically to the Lone Star State. In South Texas, in 2003 and 2004, ranchers reported seeing strange, hairless creatures on their properties that attacked and killed their animals such as chickens and goats. That all of this paralleled what was afoot on Puerto Rico inevitably provoked claims that hordes of chupacabras were on the loose—and possibly all across Texas. Whereas the Puerto Rican original was described as bipedal, glowing eyed, and winged, the monster of the

Lone Star State looked like a large, hairless dog. Which is exactly what it was—and still is.

Unlike the situation in Puerto Rico, where a specimen has never been caught or killed, in Texas it did not take long at all before a couple of the beasts were shot by irate farmers and hit by cars. A careful study of the dead animals conclusively proved they were coyotes. But they were not normal coyotes—which brings us back to the matter of shapeshifting.

In the old Native American tales, the Coyote could transform itself into numerous different creatures, even that of a person. What we saw in the 2000s, however, eerily paralleled the ancient legends, but upgraded in twenty-first-century fashion. What was thought to be severe cases of mange on the dead coyotes was nothing of the sort: the animals in question appeared to be mutating into a completely hairless offshoot of the regular south Texas coyote population. They had developed large overbites, and their front limbs were abnormally short, something that led them to run in an odd, hopping fashion. And there was the presence of curious pouches growing out of the upper parts of their hind legs. Strangest of all, several witnesses claimed to have seen the animals rise up onto their back legs and hold the position for several minutes, as they scanned the landscape.

The Texas chupacabra—which was actually something arguably even stranger—was born. And yet another layer of legend was added to the mythology surrounding the coyote and its shapeshifting skills. Ken Gerhard, a noted cryptozoologist and monster hunter, shared with me that he suspects that the strange transformation of the Texan coyote is due to mutagens—which can affect animals at a DNA level—and almost certainly sulfur dioxide, which is a by-product of coal-burning power plants. Notably, Gerhard has discovered that many sightings of these transformed coyotes have been made in the direct vicinities of Texas-based plants—something that leads him to strongly suggest this is the answer to the riddle.

So, we have a shape-changing coyote in centuries-old Native American tales, and we have exactly the same thing in twenty-first-century Texas. From the world of magic to that of science and environmental pollution, the coyote continues to shapeshift, but in very different ways.

A Black Dog and a Native American War

"Ronda" is a woman I met with in the early summer of 2007. At the time, she was living in Texas, specifically in Amarillo, located in the Lone Star State's famous Panhandle. Ronda had a very curious story to relate concerning an encounter she had in Palo Duro Canyon—or Palo Duro State Park, as it is also known. It is a huge canyon located very close to Amarillo. In 1874, a violent battle occurred in the canyon that involved the forces of the US Army—under the control of Colonel Ranald Slidell Mackenzie—and the indigenous Kiowa and Comanche Native Americans. The latter two groups suffered badly: many of them were killed and in excess of a thousand of their horses were shot dead.

According to Ronda, only a very short time before we had an initial telephone chat, she and her daughter had a very odd experience while picnicking in the heart of the canyon. The pair was having a fun time—that is, until a sense of being spied on overwhelmed them. Their instincts proved to be correct. Not far away was a huge, black dog that stared at them intently. It appeared to be a normal dog, but there was something about it that gave both mother and daughter shivers. As if on cue, the animal suddenly started to bark furiously and growled in savage fashion. And then it moved toward them. That was not a good development.

The author at Palo Duro Canyon.

As the huge hound got closer, they could see that there was something very strange about its eyes: they emanated a silvery glow. Bizarrely, the dog seemed to be walking slightly above the ground, almost as if it were floating—which is what the two women concluded is exactly what happened. Then, came the most amazing, and frightening, part of the confrontation: the large dog transformed into an equally large black cat. The two, hardly surprisingly, fled the area and watched with mouths agape as the animal vanished before their eyes.

Skinwalkers and Native Americans

In the Middle Ages, the most feared of all the many and varied shapeshifters was the werewolf, particularly so throughout much of Europe. Today, however, a very good, solid case can be made that the Skinwalker is one of the most dangerous transformers of all. It is a creature that dominates the culture and the folklore of certain Native Americans—and to the extent that some will not even utter its name, for fear of it creating a backlash against the person who dared to speak the deadly *S* word. But what, exactly, are these things that instill such fear in countless numbers of people? Let us take a look. The answers are many, but you might not be happy with what you are about to learn.

For certain Native American people, the Skinwalker—tales of which date back centuries—is a definitive witch, a crone-like thing that has the ability to change its form, and radically so, too. And it is not just one specific type of beast into which the witch can change, but multiple ones. While a shapeshifting Native American witch can take on, quite literally, hundreds of forms, the most often reported guises are bears, coyotes, various types of birds, and—at the top of the list—wolves or wolf-like animals. This latter issue, of course, emphasizes that the Skinwalker is not that dissimilar at all to the traditional European werewolf, despite being separated by distances of thousands of miles.

There can be no doubt that, in recent times, at least, interest in the Skinwalker mystery soared. In 2005, Colm A. Kelleher and George Knapp penned their best-selling book, *Hunt for the Skinwalker*. It was a book that detailed strange and terrifying activity on a remote ranch in Utah, activity that suggested manipulative Skinwalkers had descended on the ranch and quickly began wreaking havoc—maybe, simply, because they could. As well as experiencing countless UFO encounters and sightings of large and hairy Bigfoot-type beasts, the family that owned the ranch also had confrontations with a huge, malevolent wolf, a monster-sized animal upon which bullets had absolutely no effect at all.

As George Knapp noted in *Hunt for the Skinwalker*, with regard to the many and varied phenomena that caused chaos and mayhem on the ranch, "Reality isn't what it used to be."

The process by which a witch can become a Skinwalker is a highly complex one and involves several different processes. For example, witches who are both learned and skilled in magical arts can transform themselves into a wide variety of creatures, all by focusing on an image of one in their minds—very often in the confines of their teepee. In most cases, however, a witch will secure the hide of the animal they wish to become and wrap it around their shoulders and back. By effectively wearing the hide, the witch—slowly and step by step—becomes the very beast it specifically seeks to emulate. And, so certain Native American teachings maintain, this includes adopting its keen senses of smell and sight, its agility and speed, and even its complete, physical form.

Perhaps the most sinister aspect of the Skinwalker is that it has the ability to supernaturally infect people with deadly diseases and life-threatening illnesses. Strangely, on more than a few occasions, those who have found themselves in the direct, close presence of a Skinwalker have—in mere days—succumbed to very rare medical conditions. Precisely how the Skinwalker can perform such a hostile thing remains unknown. It is, however, worth noting that the Skinwalker is said to have an expert knowledge of medicine, both ancient and modern. No wonder Native Americans avoid them at all costs. And it is not just people who can fall victim to this dangerous beast. Animals—very often farm animals—have also become the targets of these multiform creatures.

For example, so-called cattle mutilations, which reached their peak in the 1970s—but are still occasionally reported to this very day—are believed by some to be the work of crazed Skinwalkers. The approach of the creatures is to remove organs and blood from cattle, specifically to use them in yet further rites and rituals designed to enhance their paranormal powers to even greater degrees. This may not be quite as strange, or as unlikely, as it might seem. Between 1975 and 1978, police officers investigating dozens of cattle mutilation events in New Mexico, Utah, Colorado, and Arizona found that many such attacks had specifically occurred on Native American reservations—something which is most assuredly food for thought.

Sedona, Arizona: the home of shapeshifters.

Of course, there is one critical issue we have yet to touch upon: namely, why would anyone even want to become a Skinwalker in the first place? The answer, as you may have already deduced, is not a good one. Adopting the guise of an animal can, quite literally, allow a person to get away with murder. After all, if the target of the Skinwalker is violently slaughtered by a rampaging bear or a savage wolf, who would even—or ever—dream of the possibility that the beast was actually a transformed human? Almost certainly not many, to be sure!

As for why the Skinwalker issue is steeped in so much mystery—despite it being the subject of a bestselling book—it is chiefly because there is a fear that speaking openly on the matter may well lead those same Skinwalkers to target them. I found this out for myself, to a graphic level, in August of 2010. I was out in the Californian desert, specifically in Joshua Tree, where—back in 1982—a spate of very savage attacks on animals occurred, amid claims that a shapeshifting Skinwalker was the culprit. In 2009 and early 2010, the attacks began yet again: vital organs were removed from the animals, as was blood, in massive amounts. My reason for being there was no coincidence: I had been hired by the VH1 channel to make a documentary on the phenomenon for the now-defunct show, *Real and Chance: The Legend Hunters*.

On the second day of shooting, the film crew and I headed out to a local animal sanctuary—which specialized in caring for, and rehabilitating, wolves. I quickly learned just how much the Skinwalker phenomenon was feared in and around Joshua Tree. And, in all likelihood, it still is. I also saw for myself a deep reluctance on the part of the staff of the sanctuary to ever utter that dreaded word. By now, you know the one I mean.

18
THE EERIE OWL PHENOMENON

OWLS HAVE A PLACE within the phenomenon of shapeshifting that goes far beyond that which many might accept as possible. They are linked to the issue of alien abductions, they pop up in numerous UFO encounters, and they appear to be far more mysterious than we can imagine. They are too, of course, a big part of the shapeshifting enigma.

There can be very few people with an interest in UFOs who have not heard of the so-called alien abduction phenomenon. The flying saucer phenomenon exploded in spectacular style in the summer of 1947 when a pilot name Kenneth Arnold encountered a number of strange, delta-shaped objects flying in formation over the Cascade Mountains in Washington State. In mere hours, UFO hysteria had begun. It reached even higher levels just one month later when the still-unresolved incident at Roswell, New Mexico, occurred. It was not until 1961, however, that the concept of alien abductions caught the attention of UFO investigators. In September of that year, Betty and Barney Hill, who lived in New Hampshire, encountered something very strange on a dark, quiet stretch of road. It was an experience that saw the Hills taken aboard a UFO and treated like definitive lab rats by emotionless, humanoid entities that seemed to have a specific interest in human reproduction. It wasn't long at all before the US Air Force, the UFO research community, and the media were looking for the truth of the strange affair. Such was the fascination with the story, writer John Fuller was commissioned to write a book on the incident, from which this brief summary was taken. Published in 1966, it was titled *The Interrupted Journey*—most apt wording.

Since that fateful night in 1961, literally thousands of people have come forward with nearly identical reports. And how many more exist—buried by witnesses who fear scorn, ridicule, and invasions of their privacy—is unknown. While the alien abduction phenomenon is multifaceted and is typified by layer upon layer of mystery, there is one specific aspect of the puzzle that has a bearing on the matter of shapeshifters—a significant bearing, too. Let us take a look at this often-overlooked angle.

In far more than a few cases of alien abduction, witnesses—or victims, take your pick—report something that is very strange but can be found all across the planet. Whether lying in their beds or driving a long, shadowy road in the woods, they have seen what they so often describe as a giant-sized owl standing at the side of the road and staring at them. There then follows a typically weird and mysterious event, one in which the witnesses suddenly find themselves aboard a UFO and subjected to the kinds of intrusive procedures reported by Betty and Barney Hill. On other occasions, however, the witness only has a vague memory of what happened to them beyond an eerie image in his or her mind of an owl with deeply penetrating eyes staring at them.

For Ufologists, the most obvious explanation is that the owl is a screen memory created by the aliens as they seek to obscure and obfuscate what really happened to the abductee. A "screen memory" is one of a nonthreatening nature that the mind and subconscious creates to mask and bury a frightening, stressful event.

It is not at all implausible, or impossible, that a highly advanced extraterrestrial species might possess the ability to create extremely visual hallucinations in the mind of the targeted abductee as part of a concerted effort to ensure that the truth of the matter never surfaced. The image of the eerie owl would overwhelm the reality of the situation, thus ensuring that the aliens' desire to stay in the shadows remained intact. Make no mistake—such cases are everywhere.

Whitley Strieber is the author of what is probably the most widely recognized book on the alien abduction phenomenon: the bestselling *Communion*, which was published in 1987, the cover of which displays a nearly hypnotic image of an alien entity. It may not be a coincidence that immediately after the first abduction experience that Strieber recalled, on December 26, 1985, his mind was filled with owl-based imagery.

Strieber's sister had her own experience with an anomalous owl in the early 1960s. Strieber wrote in *Communion* that as she drove between the Texas towns of Comfort and Kerrville after the witching hour had struck, "she was terrified to see a huge light sail down and cross the road ahead of her. A few minutes later an owl flew in front of the car. I have to wonder if that is not a screen memory, but my sister has no sense of it."

This all brings me to something else, a creature that has become a staple part of a completely different subject—cryptozoology, the study and search for unknown animals such as Bigfoot and the Loch Ness Monster. Or, based on what I'm about to share now, maybe they are not so unconnected, after all.

In 1976 the dense trees surrounding Mawnan Old Church in Cornwall, England, became a veritable magnet for a diabolical beast that was christened the Owlman. The majority of those who crossed paths with the creature asserted that it was human-like in both size and design, and possessed a pair of large wings, fiery red eyes, claws, and exuded an atmosphere of menace. No wonder people make parallels with Mothman.

It all began during the weekend of Easter 1976, when two young girls, June and Vicky Melling, had an encounter of a truly nightmarish kind in Mawnan Woods. The girls were on holiday with their parents when they saw a gigantic, feathery "bird man" hovering over the thirteenth-century church, Jonathan Downes notes in his book *The Owlman and Others.*

Since that fateful day, a handful of additional reports of the so-called Owlman have surfaced—collectively suggesting the presence in the area of a somewhat Mothman-like beast of cryptozoological or supernatural proportions, or possibly a combination of both. But now, however, there is a new angle to the mystery.

In 2016, I received an email from a woman now living in the English town of Lowestoft, but who previously lived very close to Mawnan, and specifically in the small Cornwall village of Gweek, the distance between which is approximately six and a half miles by car. It transpires that in 1998 she had a profound UFO encounter while taking the road from Mawnan to Gweek.

It was after 11:00 p.m. and the woman was driving home after visiting a friend in Mawnan. She had barely left the little village when she saw what she could only describe as a UFO, one that appeared at the side of the road—around the size of a large beach ball and glowing bright orange. The next thing she knew, she was parked at the side of the road, unable to account for around two hours of time.

But there was something else: as she came out of her groggy state, she caught sight of a huge owl-like creature that had somewhat humanoid characteristics attached to it, too. It was hovering in the air at a height of around fifteen feet but was not employing the use of its wings to keep it aloft. Given the fact that this was practically on the doorstep of where the Owlman was seen back in 1976 (and since, too), the idea that the two issues are unconnected is highly unlikely.

The witness admitted she knew of the Owlman legend. Living so close to Mawnan, it would be more astonishing had she not heard of it. There was little more she could tell me, beyond the facts surrounding the sighting of the curious ball of light, the period of missing time, and the appearance of a "humanoid owl," as I term it.

This particular encounter—which has not been publicized before—set me thinking. What if the Owlman of Cornwall is not a beast of cryptozoological proportions, after all? What if, instead, it is some strange manifestation of the UFO phenomenon, one that is designed to trick the witnesses into thinking they have encountered a large owl, when, in reality, the event was of an otherworldly nature?

This neatly dovetails into another aspect of the controversy and a pair of questions that are highly relative, even integral, to the theme of this book: What if the so-called alien Grays are not creating screen memories as a means to try and confuse them with regard to the true nature of their experiences? What if they have the ability to literally shapeshift from the form of a black-eyed extraterrestrial into that of a large owl? And, by and large, we are talking about creatures that the witnesses suggest are usually between four and five feet in height.

While some of the cases, such as that 1998 incident highlighted above, do indeed smack of a screen memory, others do not. One such encounter that falls solidly into the second category involves a

Scottish woman whom we shall refer to as "Maxine," whom I met in 2004. She lives in the Scottish town of Inverness, which is located only a very short distance from the site of yet another famous mystery: Loch Ness, the home, of course, to long-necked Nessie. As we saw earlier, it is not at all implausible that the Nessies are shape-shifters. It is, actually, all too likely.

On a clear summer day in 2007, Maxine was walking her dog along the hills that overlook Loch Ness when she saw what, from her description, can only be described as an alien Grey. When she first saw it, at a distance of a couple of hundred feet, she assumed it was a young child—chiefly because of its short height. As she got closer, and as her dog froze to the spot, she could see that not only was it not a young boy, it wasn't even human. Maxine and the Grey stared at each other for just a few seconds, after which it stretched its arms out and, in an instant, transformed into what Maxine described as an impossibly large owl: it was practically man-sized. It immediately took to the skies and headed across the loch at a fast rate. Maxine continue to watch, with astonishment, as the alien-owl thing vanished into the trees on the opposite side of the loch.

The most important aspect of Maxine's encounter is that she is 100 percent sure that she did not experience missing time. She does not have any vague memories of being taken aboard some kind of futuristic, alien craft. She is not plagued by graphic nightmares involving extraterrestrials. In fact, she is completely sure that what she recalls is exactly what she saw: a small alien creature literally shapeshifting into the form of an owl. Interestingly, since her experience took place, Maxine has come up with an intriguing theory to try to explain and rationalize the situation. She now believes that the Grays have the ability to transform their physical appearances. This, she also suggests, means that the Grays can spy on us whenever and wherever they choose, without being noticed for what they really are. If we see an owl, a black cat, a German Shepherd dog—the list goes on—we may actually be seeing something very different: a shapeshifted ET using a piece of brilliant camouflage.

A similar report comes from "Gary," of Newport Beach, California, whom I spoke with in 2014 at the Contact in the Desert conference based in Joshua Tree, California. Unlike Maxine—who has experienced just one UFO-themed incident in her entire life—Gary has had numerous encounters. His, however, are not of the alien-abduction type. For Gary, a manager at a Target store, his experiences have been of the contactee variety: face-to-face interaction with very human-looking, long-haired aliens and a wealth of interaction and discussion of a mind, body, and spirit nature.

As for Gary's experience with an owl, it occurred out at Giant Rock, California. Close to the town of Landers, Giant Rock is where, from the 1950s to the late 1970s, a famous contactee named George Van Tassel held yearly outdoor conferences on UFOs. Gary maintains that in November 2001 he rendezvoused at the old rock with an alien named Capsona—a blond-haired, beautiful woman, dressed in a long white gown. The two spent several hours discussing the precarious state of the human race. Afterward, with the sun starting to set on the desert, Capsona told Gary to back away, which he did, to a distance of about forty feet. Capsona was suddenly bathed in a white light and was transformed into a roughly four-foot-tall, brilliantly white owl, which took to the skies and was quickly lost from view.

Again, as with Maxine's experience, there was no hint of a suggestion of a screen memory. Only that of an extraterrestrial with the stunning ability to shapeshift.

19
BLOOD-SUCKING
SHAPE-CHANGERS

IN TODAY'S WORLD OF fictional vampires, the overwhelming image is that of a creature which looks like a Goth rock star or an underweight supermodel. Anemic-looking skin, black clothes, and sunken cheeks are very much the order of the day. But it wasn't always like that. Centuries ago, vampires were far more monstrous than anything that the world of Hollywood prefers to get its teeth into—pardon the pun. And, similarly, while moviemakers might occasionally still present a vampire shapeshifting into a bat, according to legend, the vampire could take on the disguise of numerous animals.

For the vast majority of people, vampires are nothing but fictional monsters designed to entertain and thrill. But long before the fictional vampire became all-dominating, there was the *real* monster. Both ancient reality and modern fantasy have one thing in common: namely, the belief that vampires thrive and survive on blood, predominantly human blood, but also that of animals, too—a process known as hematophagy. But, that is where the parallels start and finish.

It was in the early part of the nineteenth century when the vampire went from being a fairly obscure eastern European legend to a near-iconic piece of gothic literature. No, we are not talking about Bram Stoker's classic novel, *Dracula*. Although it is widely perceived and acknowledged as the definitive vampire novel, *Dracula* was somewhat of a Johnny-come-lately: it was published in 1897. It was in 1819 that the genre really began. That was the year in which John Polidori's novel *The Vampyre* surfaced. And to great acclaim, too. What Polidori did, and that Stoker expanded on, was to cast the vampire in a totally new light. This begs the question, what was that light? Well, it sure as hell wasn't the likes of *Twilight* and *True Blood*.

A careful study of ancient vampire lore and legend shows that tales of blood-drinking monsters date back millennia: they can be found in the stories and history of ancient Greece, China, and Japan. There's also no doubt that Babylonian Lilith, a hideous and dangerous creature with a predilection for invading homes in the dead of night, was what, today, very few would hesitate to call a vampire: for her, however, it was sperm, rather than blood, that she craved. Over millennia, vampies have had numerous names: *Strigoi, Vrykolakas, Empusae, Lamiae,* and *Shtriga.*

It was, however, the deadly creature of Eastern Europe, and specifically of the Middle Ages onward, that led to the development of what ultimately became today's vampire. And, certainly, "vampire" is the term that has, for at least the last few centuries, really struck a chord—it was first used to describe the terrifying blood-sucker in a 1734 publication, *The Travels of Three English Gentlemen.* This is not surprising: history has shown that from the second decade of the eighteenth century onward, tales of blood-draining—and blood-drinking—monsters proliferated throughout Austria and Serbia, with additional accounts coming out of Russia, Croatia, Poland, and Czechoslovakia. Western Europe soon fell victim to beliefs in vampires, too.

Dark tales told of frightened villagers digging up freshly buried corpses in the dead of night. Wooden stakes were plunged into hearts that no longer beat, and garlic and crosses quickly became the key tools to thwarting the deadly and bloody reign of the undead.

The vampires of the past were a grim and gruesome bunch, to be sure. Forget the rock star look: centuries ago, the blood-drinkers were easily identified by their swollen, reddish-purple faces and their overweight bodies—appearances which were attributed to the vast amounts of human blood ingested during the average attack on an unfortunate victim or several. And there was not a mouthful of large incisors anywhere in sight.

As noted earlier, the bat is the animal that most people—whether they believe in the existence of real vampires or not—associate with the vampire, when it comes to the matter of shapeshifting. Hollywood has done a very good job of emphasizing that aspect of the controversy, above all others. But, if one takes a look at what was afoot in Eastern Europe in the 1700s, one sees a very different situation. It is a situation in which the vampire has the ability to take on the form of a veritable menagerie of creatures.

The bat aside, a supernatural wolf was the vampire's most favored form of creature to transform into—something which, to a degree, blurs the lines between the vampire and the shapeshifting werewolf, which was also a monster that plagued and terrified the people of Europe centuries ago. The ancient vampire was a creature very partial to the night sky: not only would it take to a star-filled sky in the guise of a bat, it could also control the minds of both moths and owls. As was noted earlier, the owl is associated with shapeshifting, but in connection to UFOs, flying saucers, and the so-called "alien abduction" phenomenon.

Cats, foxes, rats, and sometimes a large black dog were all on the list when it came time for a vampire to change its appearance and to harness minds. The vampire was also able to increase its size and body mass, effectively turning itself into a blood-drinking Goliath. Strangest of all was the ability of the vampire to shift into a form of fog—usually a localized, but always dense and thick, fog. In view of this latter belief, it is not at all surprising that hundreds of years ago when the landscape became filled with mist and fog, fears that bands of vampires lurked within the inky depths abounded. Or that they literally *were* the fearsome fog.

Today, the vampire is near-exclusively perceived as a creature of entertainment. Way back when, however, it was a monster of terrifying proportions—one that could change its shape as easily and as quickly as we might blink an eye. Keep that in mind if, late on one dark and misty night, you see a large bat and a wolf coming toward you through a dense fog. The old legends may not just be legends after all.

The Vampire of the Islands

Of all the many and various shapeshifters that populate our planet, in the terror stakes there are very few that can rival the horrific *Aswang* of the Philippines. A murderous thing that haunts the woods and jungles of the islands, it has certain attributes that will, by now, have become acutely familiar. They include a strong rotting odor and an ability to change into the form of an upright wolf and that of a huge black dog with glowing, red eyes. Appropriately for a creature that has multiple forms, it also has more than a few names, including the *Sok-Sok* and the *Tik-Tik*. The odd titles are derived from ancient legends that maintain they are the click-like noises the Aswangs make when they are about to launch an attack on the doomed and the unwary.

Although the Aswang is recognized as being a creature that lurks in the hearts of numerous islands in the Philippines, the overwhelming majority of all the reports on record surface from the island of Mindanao, which has a population in excess of twenty million. Just like the Kushtaka of Alaska, the Aswang is noted for its nausea-inducing smell and its sore-covered body. Unlike the Kushtaka, however, the Aswang is often seen wearing clothes—albeit almost always ripped and tattered. And whereas the Kushtaka are both male and female, in most cases the Aswang is described as being female. In contrast to the beautiful woman that Scotland's Kelpie can turn into, however, the Aswang is almost always described as being a hag-like, ugly creature of grotesque proportions.

Unfortunately for their victims, and regardless of their near-decaying appearances, Aswangs are said to be phenomenal athletes. They can run at incredible speeds and are able to climb trees and scale rooftops with incredible ease—something that is made even easier by their shape-changing abilities. Children and babies are particular delicacies of the Aswangs, who will seek out the young whenever and wherever possible when hunger strikes.

One of the most disturbing aspects of the Aswang legend maintains that if a person receives a bite from such a creature but is not outright killed in the process, the person will then become an Aswang. And very quickly, too. They will turn homicidal, their skin will decay, and they will take on a decidedly dead-looking appearance. And let us not forget that vomit-inducing smell, too.

In light of this, it could justifiably be said that the Aswang phenomenon is the Philippines' very own equivalent of a zombie apocalypse, one of the kind most graphically portrayed in the likes of the Armageddon-driven *The Walking Dead*, *World War Z*, and *Night of the Living Dead*. Except for one important thing: unlike the Aswang of the Philippines, in the hugely popular movies and television series the reanimated dead don't have the ability to transform into human-like wolves or dogs resembling the rampaging monster portrayed in the pages of *The Hound of the Baskervilles*.

Puerto Rico's Notorious Shape-Changer

In August 1995, the Canóvanas region of the island of Puerto Rico was hit by a spate of very bizarre attacks on farm animals. The unfortunate creatures—typically goats, chickens, and pigs—were found dead with deep puncture wounds to their necks and amid claims that significant amounts of blood were missing from their corpses. Farmers were on edge, the media had an absolute field day, and the people of Puerto Rico were plunged into states that ranged from fear to hysteria. When similar killings began to be reported in numerous other parts of Puerto Rico, that fear was amplified to even greater levels. All of which is hardly surprising, when one takes into consideration the physical appearance of the beast that was believed to be behind all of the slaughtering.

The first person—so far as we know—to see the beast was a woman named Madelyne Tolentino, who lived in Canóvanas, the initial scene of all the action, and whose story is told in Ben Radford's 2011 book, *Tracking the Chupacabra*. She described it as a fairly compact animal that ran on two legs—in a strange hopping style—and that had what looked like a row of feathers running down the back of its head and spine. As media interest grew and grew, so did sightings of the mysterious monster. That's when things became not just interesting, but *beyond* interesting. There is a very good reason for that: not everyone saw the same beast that Tolentino encountered. Or, at least, it did not look the same.

It is one thing to suggest that, in the 1990s, one unknown and dangerous animal was on the loose in Puerto Rico. It is quite another, however, to suggest that multiple strange creatures were running wild on the island. And, yet, that appears to have been exactly what was going on. Unless all of the reports were of the same monster. But, given their physical differences, how could that be true? Very easily, that is how, if the chupacabra is a shapeshifter. As amazing as it may sound, a significant amount of data points in that specific direction.

Puerto Rico, where the chupacabra roams.

Although the first sighting of the creature in the summer of 1995 effectively dictated how the locals perceived the animal to look, not everyone reported something that resembled the monster seen by Madelyne Tolentino, as we shall now see. In the days, weeks, months—and even years—that followed, countless reports of chupacabra attacks on farm animals were reported. The problem, however, is that the descriptions of the beast varied to incredible degrees.

In some cases, witnesses told of seeing an animal that did not have the feathery line running along the back of its head, neck, and spine, as described by Tolentino. Instead, they saw a row of menacing spikes, which stood erect and around four to five inches in length. And, of course, it would be very hard to mistake a line of feathers for a row of vicious spikes!

Then, there was the matter of how the animal ran. According to both Tolentino and the majority of the early witnesses, it was a bipedal beast, albeit one which bounced along in a bizarre hopping fashion. Others, however, were sure that the creatures they saw ran on four limbs. And there was nothing bizarre about its movements: they were likened to the way in which a large cat—such as a mountain lion—would stalk its prey. Now, let us take a look at the eyes of the chupacabra. Some sightings involved creatures with bright blue eyes. In other cases, the eyes were a piercing, devilish red and glowing.

The most significant factor, however, was the matter of the wings of the chupacabra. Yes, that is correct—*wings*. In some cases, but most certainly not all, the creatures were said to have had large and powerful-looking bat-like wings. In other words, they were black and leathery. When faced with such stories, other witnesses swore the monsters had absolutely no wings at all. Adding to the puzzle is the fact that on my second expedition to seek out the Puerto Rican chupacabra, I spoke with a man named Pucho who saw such a thing, but it had wings like those of a large bird: they were feathery.

Most controversial of all are the reports of the chupacabra transforming into a large and lumbering Bigfoot! I should stress that such reports are rare and few and far between. However, I do have eleven such reports in my files. In all the cases, the witnesses saw the chupacabra engulfed by a near-blinding white light and then mutating into a large, hair-covered humanoid before their startled eyes.

When we put all of this information together, we are clearly faced with a major conundrum: How can one creature take on multiple appearances and forms? Well, the answer is that no normal animal can do such a thing. But, there is nothing normal about the chupacabra. Rather, everything suggests it is undeniably abnormal.

On all of my many trips to Puerto Rico, I have heard several oft-repeated theories for what the beasts are or may be. The list includes alien beings, giant bats, and the products of secret labs run by scientists engaging in bizarre genetic, cloning, and gene-splicing experiments. And there is one more theory: the chupacabras were invoked or conjured up by clandestine groups that engage in the black arts and are directly responsible for creating a portal, or what we might call a supernatural doorway, that lets the monsters enter our world at will. There is no doubt at all that Puerto Rico is home to multiple cults and secret societies that engage in animal sacrifice, ritual magic, and occult practices. I know this because I have had the opportunity to speak with a few of them. They are dangerous and powerful bodies, ones not to be crossed.

The most likely scenario to explain the nature and presence of the Puerto Rican chupacabra, however, is that it is the shapeshifting denizen of another realm of existence. It is a monster that, when called forth, eagerly made a new home—as well as an entirely new hunting ground—on the island and has no intention of returning to the weird realm from which it first surfaced.

20
A CATALOG OF CREEPY CRITTERS

NOW, IN OUR FINAL chapter, we will address a few strange and mysterious shapeshifters: one is the fox, the second is a famous, glowing-eyed beast of the skies, the third is the hyena, and the fourth is a hideous reptile. In their own unique ways, they all have a place in the shapeshifter menagerie.

Japan has its very own shapeshifter: the *kitsune*. It is a word that means "fox." Japanese lore has long maintained that each and every fox that lives—and has ever lived—has the ability to take on the appearance of a human, whether that of a man or of a woman. And, like many of the shapeshifters that we have focused on so far, the kitsune alternates from being a malevolent creature to a placid and helpful entity. Mostly, however, it acts as a classic Trickster—manipulating people and playing endless mind games. Those kitsune that portray a positive nature are known as *zenko*, while those that border upon the downright dangerous are termed *yako*. The former will often hide food and various household items, something that has the victim endlessly and frustratingly looking for assumedly misplaced things. The dangerous ones, however, seek out the unwary and lead them into potentially deadly and treacherous places, such as bogs, marshes, and cascading rivers.

The stories of the Japanese kitsune were actually inspired by the folklore and mythology of China, where tales of supernatural foxes abounded thousands of years ago. It was the stories of these paranormal foxes—known in China as the *Huli Jing*—that soon became adapted and expanded on by the Japanese. The kitsune is said to be a spirit-based entity. Not of the kind that has returned from the grave in ethereal form, but as an entity that has paranormal qualities and powers and is spiritual in terms of its outlook. As for their physical appearances, the kitsune look like regular foxes. Except for one thing: they can have up to nine tails.

As for its shapeshifting skills, they are both many and varied. We have seen that beautiful women turn up time and time again when it comes to the matter of morphing entities. The Scottish kelpie, the demonic succubus, and even strange balls of light have taken on the appearances of highly attractive, alluring women. The kitsune is no different: women and teenage girls are among its most popular disguise, as is sometimes the form of a wrinkled old man. As for how, exactly, the shapeshifting occurs, here is where things get *very* weird. To allow a transformation to take place, the kitsune is required to carefully place a handful of reeds on its head. And then, lo, the process of morphing quickly results.

It is not just the form of people that the kitsune can take on. Like the dryad of ancient Greece, the kitsune can turn itself into a tree—and into the image of the moon, too. A variation on all the above maintains that as well as taking on the form of a woman or a girl, the kitsune can also possess the minds of both—in very much the same fashion as demonic possession. All of which reveals the sheer bizarre nature of this incredible shapeshifter.

Mothman—Disaster at the Bridge

There are certain strange creatures that just about everyone has heard of. They include the Loch Ness Monster, Bigfoot, the Abominable Snowman, and the chupacabra. And there is one more strange entity that has become a definitive icon in the field of monster lore. Its name: Mothman. Although the story of Mothman has its origins in the 1960s, the vast majority of people were not exposed to the story until 2002. That was when a movie on the mystery surfaced. It was titled *The Mothman Prophecies* and starred Richard Gere, and it was based upon John Keel's book, *The Mothman Prophecies*. There are solid reasons to believe that Mothman is a creature with the ability to shapeshift—and into more than one form. But, first, a bit of background on the monster is required.

The author poses with Point Pleasant's Mothman in September 2016.

Point Pleasant, West Virginia, is a city of around four and a half thousand people. In 1774, the city became the site of a now-historic battle between the forces of Colonel Andrew Lewis and Native Americans from the Shawnee and Mingo groups and was overseen by Shawnee Chief Cornstalk. It was a bloody and violent battle that Cornstalk's people lost. Despite the historic nature of the battle, there is no doubt that it has been eclipsed by a series of events that occurred between November 1966 and December 1967: the reign of Mothman.

It all began on November 12, 1966, as Keel notes in his book. On the night in question, a large, humanoid figure was seen—somewhat appropriately—in the heart of a local graveyard. The witnesses, a group of workmen, described the beast as being brown in color and sporting a pair of large wings. The legend had duly begun. And it had no intention of stopping. Seventy-two hours later, the Mothman was seen again, this time by Steve and Mary Mallette and Roger and Linda Scarberry. At the time, they were driving around an area known locally as the TNT plant. Its official title, however, was the West Virginia Ordnance Works—today, called the McClintic Wildlife Management Area—a place at which TNT was manufactured and stored during the Second World War. The volatile material was stored in large igloo-like structures that, today, are overgrown by trees and bushes, and which give off a decidedly weird vibe when one walks around them—particularly so at night.

For the Scarberrys and the Mallettes, all young at the time, it was just a typical night, one spent cruising around the plant, having fun, and hanging out, noted Keel. That all changed when all four saw a pair of what appeared to be bright red eyes peering out of the surrounding darkness. Curiosity quickly became overwhelming fear when the two couples realized that the eyes were attached to a large figure, around seven feet in height, with large, powerful wings.

The author explores one of
Point Pleasant's long-abandoned TNT storage areas.

All four quickly realized it was time to flee the area—which they did. The accelerator was pushed to the floor, and they raced back to the heart of the town—with the winged monster pursuing them every step of the way. Trying to shake off the flying beast proved to be a hopeless task: it doggedly chased them for miles. They quickly headed to the police station, at which point the monster soared away into the darkness. It was clear to the police that this was no prank: all four were chilled to the bone and in deep states of stress and anxiety. Statements were made and a file was opened—not unlike a definitive X-File, one might say. To the horror of everyone, this was not the end of things. Mothman was back soon. Very soon.

As December 1966 loomed large on the horizon, a man named Thomas Ury encountered Mothman while driving past a field on Route 62, which is situated north of the old TNT plant. He too described the red-eyed beast as humanoid in shape and gray (rather than brown) in color, and it took to the skies in a very strange fashion: instead of flapping its wings like a bird or a bat, it stretched out its wings and rose vertically into the air—an action that Ury likened to the rise of a helicopter. Unfortunately for Ury, Mothman had clearly seen him; that much was evidenced by the fact that it quickly pursued him, and in much the same way it had the Scarberrys and the Mallettes a couple of weeks earlier. Ruth Foster—from Charleston—had the misfortune to come face to face with Mothman only days later. Once again the fiery eyes and large wings dominated the story. Attempts to explain everything away as owls, cranes, and large birds of prey were immediately dismissed as ridiculous by the witnesses.

Perhaps inevitably, when the media got into the controversy, just about everyone in and around Point Pleasant was talking about the creature, as Mothman authorities Jeff Wamsley and Donnie Sergent Jr. noted in their book, *Mothman: The Facts Behind the Legend*. They weren't just discussing it, however: they were out at the TNT plant and amid the thick woods looking for it. And in their droves, too. The Point Pleasant Police were neither pleased nor amused by the situation, which threatened to spiral out of control. A warning was put out that anyone found carrying a gun around the plant would be arrested on site. Sightings of Mothman continued as 1966 gave way to 1967. Reports of UFO activity abounded and even the dreaded Men in Black were seen, turning up on doorsteps late at night and warning people not to talk about their encounters with Mothman. Point Pleasant was, by now, a place gripped and overwhelmed by fear, panic, and paranoia. That was nothing compared to the events that occurred in December 1967, however. Death and overwhelming tragedy were just around the corner.

It was on the night of the fifteenth that Point Pleasant's huge Silver Bridge reached breaking point and plunged into the waters of the Ohio River, killing dozens of people in the process. It is notable that although Mothman did not vanish after the terrible events of December 15, reports certainly dropped off significantly.

The people of Point Pleasant have not forgotten Mothman, the many and varied encounters with the beast, or the collapse of the bridge and the unfortunate souls whose lives were lost on that fateful night. Each and every year, the town holds the Mothman Festival. It is a hugely popular event, one that attracts thousands of visitors. In 2016—the fiftieth anniversary of the first Mothman encounter—the festival attracted more than 10,000 people, all of them eager and excited to buy Mothman T-shirts, keyrings, fridge magnets, books, paintings, and even pancakes and burgers! Local bands and a Miss Mothman pageant added to the entertainment. The specter of death and tragedy still haunts the area, however.

Today, there are two primary theories for Mothman's presence in Point Pleasant during the 1960s. Some researchers of the phenomenon view Mothman as a Grim Reaper–type entity, one that provokes tragedy and loss of life. Others, however, are of the opinion that Mothman specifically manifested to warn people of the looming disaster. Whatever the truth, Mothman is now as much a part of American folklore as it is an integral entity of monster hunting. All of which brings us to the matter of shapeshifting.

While the classic image of Mothman is that of a large, humanoid entity with blazing red eyes, not everyone has described the creature in such a fashion. In September 2016, I drove to Point Pleasant with good friend and fellow creature-seeker Ken Gerhard and Ken's girlfriend, Jen Devillier. We were there to attend and speak at the Mothman Festival. While we were in town we received a number of accounts that presented Mothman in a very different light. Yes, witnesses told us of seeing the classic imagery that has now become famous. It is illuminating to note, however, that some reports were very different.

I received a report of a creature seen at the site of the old, long-collapsed bridge that resembled the legendary Thunderbird of Native American folklore—a gigantic, eagle-like bird noted for its dazzling, colored feathers. In sharp contrast, an elderly woman—also at the Mothman Festival—told me of how she had seen what she believed to have been Mothman out at the TNT area in 1971 but that it eerily resembled a pterodactyl, a flying reptile that existed 228 to 66 million years ago from Triassic to the Cretaceous Period. It may come as a surprise to many to learn that reports of flying monsters that have a distinct pterodactyl-type appearance surface regularly, every year, across the United States—and particularly so on the Texas-Mexico border.

It scarcely needs saying that the idea that this might be the home of multiple flying monsters—such as a brown-colored humanoid, a gray-hued and manlike thing, a pterodactyl, and a Native American Thunderbird—stretches credulity to the breaking point. Far more likely, we are dealing with a supernatural entity that can take on the appearance of multiple flying enigmas—some of a very human-type appearance and others that are far more animal-like in appearance. Plus, we have already seen how so many shapeshifters are linked to death, tragedy, and to bridges, too. Mothman is also a creature that is linked to disaster, mayhem, extinguished lives, and bridges. A shifter of the skies? To be sure, yes.

Africa's Horrific Hyena

In very much the same way that the United Kingdom is home to the eerie Phantom Black Dog and the United States has the morphing and mysterious coyote, so the continent of Africa has its very own equivalent. It is known as the were-hyena—a creature that some believe is a human who becomes a hyena, while others teach that it is a hyena with the ability to take on human form. Before we get to the matter of the supernatural hyena, let us first take a look at its regular, normal equivalent.

Widespread across East Africa and South Africa, the hyena is a formidable and highly dangerous animal, one that will not think twice about attacking, killing, and even eating people if it comes down to it. Muscular and athletic, the hyena can reach a height of around three feet and can live for up to twenty-five years. Now, we'll examine the far stranger side of the hyena—the one that is dominated by shapeshifting.

As far as the morphing beast of Africa is concerned, it is East Africa and North Africa where the creature is predominantly said to dwell. One of the most visible of the various bodies of African were-hyenas is that which is known as the *Bultungin*. It lurks and voraciously hunts in the vicinity of Lake Chad, which borders upon northern Nigeria. In 1883, Gerald Massey wrote of this particular controversy in *The Natural Genesis*: "In the Kanuri language of Bornu (Africa), the name of the hyena is *Bultu*, and from this is formed the verb *bultungin*, which signifies 'I transform myself into a hyena.' There is a town named Kabultinoa, the inhabitants of which are said to possess this faculty of transformation."

Massey was of the opinion that this belief could be explained away in wholly down-to-earth fashion, and as a result of "the donning of the hyena skin in their religious masquerade." But is that all there is to it, rites and rituals? According to the locals, it's not. Far from it. Throughout Morocco, the Lake Chad area, and Tanzania, there is an intriguing belief that each and every blacksmith has the ability to take on the form of a hyena—chiefly as a result of the same blacksmiths also being experts in the fields of magic and sorcery. Whereas the werewolf traditionally surfaces when the moon is full, the blacksmith-turned-were-hyena is limited to activity during daylight hours. Interestingly, in Tanzania there is a longstanding belief that witches travel on the backs of supernatural spotted hyenas late at night and in much the same fashion that the traditional European witch takes to the skies on the traditional broomstick.

Moving on, we have the were-hyena of the Republic of Mali, in West Africa. The republic is home to a secret society known as the *Kore*. Jurgen W. Frembgen says in "The Magicality of the Hyena: Beliefs and Practices in West and South Asia" that members of the society, "'become' hyenas by using zoomorphic helmet masks and playing dramatic roles, both of which refer to the dirty habits, trickiness, and nastiness of the animal mentioned above; they may also be used to invoke fear among the participants."

Real shapeshifting hyenas or tales born out of graphic, violent rites? The question remains wide open.

Reptiles of the Royal Kind

There's no doubt that when it comes to the matter of conspiracy theories, there is one controversial claim that just about beats all the rest. It's the assertion that the British royal family is nothing less than deadly, bloodthirsty, shapeshifting monsters. "Bloodthirsty" is a very apt word to use, since the royals are said to quaff on human blood just about as enthusiastically as the rest of the British population likes to knock back pints of beer in their local pub. They are shapeshifters with incredible power and influence—so we are told.

Welcome to the world of the Reptilians—interdimensional monsters seven to eight feet tall that masquerade as people but are anything but. At least, that's how the story goes. There's one person to thank (if that's the correct term to use!) for bringing this strange and enduring claim to light. His name is David Icke. Once a well-known goalkeeper for Coventry City—an English soccer team—Icke is, today, a leading light in the shadowy domains where the conspiracy-minded and the paranoid hang out. His books include *The Biggest Secret* and *The David Icke Guide to the Global Conspiracy*.

Are Queen Elizabeth II, her husband, Prince Philip (Duke of Edinburgh), and the heir to the throne, Prince Charles, really monsters that are either an ancient species that originate right here on earth or extraterrestrials from a faraway world? We'll start with the first theory. According to those who adhere to this particular theory, the royal family is at the top of the pile when it comes to the matter of who really owns and runs the planet.

Forget presidents and prime ministers, the real secret forces that control and manipulate our world are the Babylonian Brotherhood (discussed in Icke's book *The Biggest Secret*), an ancient race of dangerous shapeshifters that were responsible for ancient tales of the likes of Quetzalcoatl, whose name means "feathered serpent." He was a significant deity-like force in Mesoamerica and first surfaced around 100 BCE. He is also said to have been an entity that brought science and farming to the culture of that era and area. Although, given the apparent hatred that the Reptilians have for us, the likelihood is that Quetzalcoatl's actions were self-serving and were designed to keep people in their place and under his firm and cold-hearted control and sway.

It's intriguing to note that almost three thousand years ago, the ancient people of Mexico had other serpent-based gods—all of which has helped to nurture the idea that yesterday's reptilian deities are still among us and are just about as widespread as they were way back when. Today, however, their influence is not just in Mesoamerica, but all across the world, and even in the domain of politics, too. That's right: it's not just the British royal family who the conspiracy-minded believe are monsters.

The author and the Reptilian-like
creature from the Black Lagoon.

Leading Reptilians are said to include the Clintons (Bill and Hillary), Henry Kissinger—a former US Secretary of State and a National Security Advisor—and President George W. Bush. Oh, and lest we forget, the late Hollywood legend Bob Hope, too. Yes, really. Or not.

One of those who helped bring this matter to the attention of the conspiracy-obsessed—and, in quick time, to both the media and popular culture, too—was a Californian woman named Arizona Wilder, who claims to have been mind-controlled and manipulated by the likes of the world's most infamous secret society, the dreaded and feared Illuminati. Wilder's claims get even, ahem, wilder. She maintains she has witnessed diabolical human sacrifice at the hands of the Rockefellers, the Rothschilds, members of the Bush family (yes, those Bushes) and at least one pope. As for Queen Elizabeth II, well …

Certainly, Arizona Wilder's most graphic and controversial claim is that she witnessed the Queen partake in such sacrifices and eat the flesh and drink the blood of her unfortunate human victims. On one occasion, said Wilder, Queen Elizabeth was so fired up that she practically tore out a poor soul's throat, drinking down the blood as it spewed forth. According to Wilder, in her reptilian form the queen has skin that is a pale, sickly color. Her face, meanwhile, changes into something that closely resembles a beak.

Adding even more to this story is Wilder's claim that, back in 1981, she met with Lady Diana, then very soon to become Diana, Princess of Wales. According to Wilder, the Princess was forced to take part in a ritual of ancient and secret proportions, one that involved the Queen, Prince Philip, and Prince Charles and his lover and now wife, Camilla Parker Bowles. Placed into a drugged-out state, Diana was told that there was one reason, and one reason only, for the marriage: to ensure that the Royal Reptilian blood-line continued. When Diana was tragically killed in Paris, France, in 1997—admittedly, an incident still shrouded in mystery and intrigue years later—Icke wove her untimely death into his Reptilian scenario.

Conspiracy-theorists who fully believed the Reptilian scenario practically foamed at the mouth when Mohamed Al-Fayed—the father of Dodi Fayed, who was Diana's boyfriend at the time of her death and who died with her in the terrible car crash that took three lives—referred to Camilla Parker Bowles as Prince Charles's "crocodile wife." It was a statement the BBC highlighted in an online article of February 2008 titled "Diana murdered, Al Fayed claims." Then, when Fayed labeled the entire Royal Family as the "Dracula family," (noted in Paul Majendie's 2008 article for Reuters) it only added to the idea that the Royals were copious drinkers of human blood. Was Dodi Fayed—in a slightly less than subtle fashion—trying to warn people of the growing reptilian threat in the midst of just about everyone?

Today, the so-called Reptilian agenda terrifies, intrigues, and entertains nearly endless numbers of people. And it's a phenomenon that clearly isn't going away anytime soon. Are the numerous people who make up the British royal family shapeshifting reptiles with origins that date back millennia? Is the entire issue nothing but the likes of fabrication, lies, pranks, and jokes? Or does it hazily lie somewhere in between? It all depends on who you ask—as is the case with practically all conspiracy theories of a highly bizarre nature.

CONCLUSION

NOW, WITH OUR STORY at its end, it is time for us to try to make some sense of this strange and sinister band of supernatural entities: Who, or what, are they? What are their motivations? Are they entirely separate from each other—shapeshifting being the only thing that connects them—or are they somehow all part of one specific phenomenon? They are questions that get right to the heart of the puzzle.

When we address all of these strange, sinister, and so often highly dangerous things, we see an undeniable pattern that links each and every one of them. It is a pattern that revolves around the manipulation of the human mind, bridges, cemeteries, woods, bodies of water, and the plunging of countless people into bizarre situations that provoke stress, paranoia, and insanity—sometimes even death. Trying to place each of these things—whether kelpies, Men in Black, djinn, Phantom Black Dogs, Alien Big Cats, weird balls of light, and so on—into completely different categories does not work. And the reason why it doesn't work is because it cannot work.

As we have seen, the parallels, the nearly identical traits, and the sinister motivations of all of these things are so incredibly similar that we are forced to come to one astonishing conclusion: each and every shapeshifter is a part of a single phenomenon. They are whatever they want to be, whenever and wherever they want to be.

Shapeshifters are not our friends. They are not here to help us, even if they assure us they are. Avoid them at all costs. Or else.

BIBLIOGRAPHY

Chapter 1: Werewolves of the Past

"August 1972 'Wolfman' of Defiance." News of the Strange. Accessed 2016. http://www.oocities.org/zoomar1/wolfman.html.

Bartsch, Karl. "The Werewolf of Klein-Krams." In *Werewolf Legends from Germany* by D. L. Ashliman. Pittsburgh: University of Pittsburgh, 1997. Accessed 2016. http://www.pitt.edu/~dash/werewolf.html#bartsch183.

Conjure, Doc. "The Defiance OH Werewolf." *The Demoniacal* (blog), October 24, 2012. http://thedemoniacal.blogspot.com/2012/10/the-defiance-oh-werewolf.html.

O'Donnell, Elliot. *Werewolves*. London, UK: Methuen, 1912.

Saxby, Jessie Margaret. *Traditional Shetland Lore*. Edinburgh, Scotland: Grant & Murray, Ltd., 1932.

Schöppner, Alexander. *The Legend of the Bavarian Lands*. Hanover, Germany: Hansebooks, 2016.

———. "The Wolf Stone." In *Werewolf Legends from Germany* by D. L. Ashliman. Pittsburgh: University of Pittsburgh, 1997.

Accessed 2016. http://www.pitt.edu/~dash/werewolf.html #wolfstone.

"Scottish Myths: Wulver the Kindhearted Shetland Werewolf." *The Scotsman,* February 9, 2016. http://www.scotsman.com/heritage/people-places/scottish-myths-wulver-the-kindhearted-shetland-werewolf-1-4025249.

Shuker, Karl. "Wulvers and Wolfen and Werewolves, Oh My!!—Tales of the Uninvited." *ShukerNature* (blog), July 28, 2012. http://karlshuker.blogspot.com/2012/07/wulvers-and-wolfen-and-werewolves-oh-my.html.

Stegall, James. "Werewolf Case in Defiance Not Viewed Lightly by Police." *The Blade* (Toledo, OH), August 2, 1972.

Summers, Montague. *The Werewolf.* Secaucus, NJ: Citadel Press, 1973.

Chapter 2: The Horrors of Hexham

Ferol, Stuart. "The Hexham Wolf." *Fortean Times* 294 (November 2012): 42–47.

My Good Babushka. "The Girt Dog of Ennerdale." Democratic Underground. May 31, 2016. http://www.democraticunderground.com/1018869900.

Robins, Don. "The Hexham Heads." *Alpha* 8 (1980) 8–9.

Rothery, Emily. "The Tale of the Mysterious Girt Dog of Ennerdale." Lancashire Life. April 3, 2015. http://www.lancashirelife.co.uk/out-about/pets/the_tale_of_the_mysterious_girt_dog_of_ennerdale_1_4020788.

Screeton, Paul. *Quest for the Hexham Heads.* Woolsery, UK: CFZ Press, 2012.

———. *Tales of the Hexham Heads.* Self-published, 1980.

Williams, Paul. *Howls of Imagination: Wolves of England*. Loughborough, UK: Heart of Albion Press, 2007.

Chapter 3: Shapeshifting at the Cemetery

"Cannock Chase Werewolves, West Midlands, England." Ghost-Story.co.uk. Accessed 2016. http://www.ghost-story.co.uk/index.php/other-paranormal/188-cannock-chase-werewolves-west-midlands-england.

Edge, Kevin. "Werewolf Spotted in Cannock." *Stafford (England) Post*, April 26, 2007.

Sentinel. "20 Sightings of a Werewolf at Cannock Chase." *Sentinel* (Stoke, UK), March 22, 2015. http://www.stokesentinel.co.uk/20-sightings-werewolf-cannock-chase/story-26212758-detail/story.html.

"Werewolves in Staffordshire." Odd Staffordshire. BBC. http://www.bbc.co.uk/stoke/content/articles/2009/09/29/werewolves_in_staffs_feature.shtml. September 29, 2009.

Wes. Comment on "Do Werewolves Roam the Woods of England?" by Nick Redfern. *There's Something in the Woods* (blog), May 17, 2007. http://monsterusa.blogspot.com/2007/05/do-werewolves-roam-woods-of-england.html?showComment=1179533040000#c7882864213802842158.

West Midlands Ghost Club. "But I'm Alright Naaoooooowww-wwww!!!!!" *West Midlands Ghost Club* (blog), October 1, 2009. http://westmidlandsghostclub.blogspot.com/2009/10/but-im-alright-naaoooooowwwwwww.html.

Chapter 4: Bridge Beasts

Burne, Charlotte. *Shropshire Folk-Lore: A Sheaf of Gleanings*. London, UK: Trubner & Co., 1883.

"Ghostly Guide to the Shropshire Union Canal." Canal and River Trust. Last modified November 29, 2016. https://canalriver trust.org.uk/news-and-views/features/ghostly-guide-to-the -shropshire-union-canal.

Haworth, Jessica, and Mark Branagan. "Mystery 'Werewolf' Creature Terrifying Families in Hull Sparks Major Hunt." *Daily Mirror*, May 16, 2016. http://www.mirror.co.uk/news/weird-news /mystery-werewolf-creature-terrifying-families-7979525.

"The Legend of the Donkey Lady." Weird US. Accessed 2016. http://www.weirdus.com/states/texas/local_legends/donkey _lady_bridge/.

Mayes, Michael. "The Legend of the 'Donkey Lady' of San Antonio." *Texas Cryptid Hunter* (blog), February 18, 2014. http:// texascryptidhunter.blogspot.com/2014/02/the-legend-of -donkey-lady-of-san-antonio.html.

Mills, Jen. "Townspeople Gather to Hunt Werewolf in Hull Known as 'Old Stinker.'" *Metro,* May 15, 2016. http://metro. co.uk/2016/05/15/townspeople-gather-to-hunt-werewolf-in- hull-known-as-old-stinker-5883952/.

Moon, Jim. "Folklore on Friday—Monkey Business on the Union Canal." *The Moon Lens* (blog), February 26, 2016. http:// hypnogoria.blogspot.com/2016/02/folklore-on-friday -monkey-business-on.html.

Ware, Jessica. "The Werewolf of Hull! Witnesses Claim They've Spotted 8ft Tall Fanged Beast with Human-like Features Nicknamed 'Old Stinker.'" *Daily Mail,* May 15, 2016. http://www .dailymail.co.uk/news/article-3591219/Hull-residents-spot -fanged-beast-human-like-features-nicknamed-Old-Stinker .html.

Chapter 5: Shape-Changers of the Water

Hope, Robert Charles. *The Legendary Lore of the Holy Wells of England, Including Rivers, Lakes, Fountains and Springs*. London, UK: Elliot Stock Books, 1893.

"The Each Uisge (Water Horse)." Loch Ness Water. Accessed 2016. http://www.lochnesswater.co.uk/nessie_monster_mythology.htm.

Johnson, Ben. "The Kelpie." Historic UK. Accessed 2016. http://www.historic-uk.com/CultureUK/The-Kelpie/.

"North East Shropshire." Inside Shropshire: Shropshire Promotions. Accessed 2016. http://www.shropshire-promotions.co.uk/NE-2.html.

Watson, Roland. *The Water Horses of Loch Ness*. CreateSpace Independent Publishing Platform, 2011.

Chapter 6: Dogs of the Paranormal Kind

BBC News. "Beast of Dartmoor 'Is My Pet Dog.'" August 3, 2007. http://news.bbc.co.uk/2/hi/uk_news/england/devon/6929397.stm.

"Bowerman's Nose." Dartmoor Walks. Accessed 2016. http://www.richkni.co.uk/dartmoor/bower.htm.

Burchell, Simon. *Phantom Black Dogs in Latin America*. Loughborough, UK: Heart of Albion Press, 2007.

Doyle, Arthur Conan. *The Hound of the Baskervilles*. London, UK: Cox & Wyman, Ltd., 1961.

Faery Folklorist. "Wisht Hounds Part 1—Wistman's Wood." *The Faery Folklorist* (blog), October 4, 2011. http://faeryfolklorist.blogspot.com/2011/10/wisht-hounds-part-1-wistmans-wood.html.

Register. "Dog with a Human Face." June 15, 1905.

Rowlands, Samuel. *The Discovery of a London Monster, called The Blacke Dogg of Newgate: Profitable for All Readers to Take Heed By.* EEBO Editions, 2010.

Salkeld, Luke. "That's Not the Beast of Dartmoor … It's My Pet Dog." *Daily Mail,* August 23, 2007. http://www.dailymail.co .uk/news/article-472909/Thats-Beast-Dartmoor--pet-dog .html.

"Strange Animal: Has an Almost Human Face and a Red Mustache." *Pittsburgh Press,* May 3, 1905. Google News. https:// news.google.com/newspapers?nid=1144&dat=19050503 &id=uAgbAAAAIBAJ&sjid=qUgEAAAAIBAJ&pg=1059, 6105628&hl=en.

Trubshaw, Bob, ed. *Explore Phantom Black Dogs.* Loughborough, UK: Heart of Albion Press, 2005.

Chapter 7: Witches and Shapeshifting

Arnold, Neil. "The Warrington Man-Beast!" *Monster! The A–Z of Zooform Phenomena* (blog). August 19, 2011. http://zooform .blogspot.com/2011/08/warrington-man-beast.html.

Barnes, Wally. *Ghosts, Mysteries & Legends of Old Warrington.* Wigan, UK: Owl Books, 1990.

Magic. "Cat Familiar." *Witches Lore,* (blog), March 19, 2010. http://witcheslore.com/bookofshadows/magical-creatures -bookofshadows/cat-familiar/219/.

Martin, Patricia J. "Animals and Witchcraft (The Witches Familiar): Rabbits & Hares." Controverscial.com. February 27, 2009. http://www.controverscial.com/Animals%20and%20 Witchcraft%20-%20Rabbits%20and%20Hares.htm.

Mastin, Luke. "Famous Witches—Isobel Gowdie (?–1662)."
Witchcraft: A Guide to the Misunderstood and Maligned. 2009.
http://www.witchcraftandwitches.com/witches_gowdie.html.

Tinker, Fiona. "Isobel Gowdie." Witches' Voice. August 29, 2010.
http://www.witchvox.com/va/dt_va.html?a=ukgb6&c=words
&id=14052.

"The Witch's Familiar." Wiccan Magick. Accessed 2016. http://
wiccanmagick69.tripod.com/id15.html.

Chapter 8: The Black Cat Phenomenon

"1900–1950: The Leopard Society in 'Vai Country,' in Bassaland."
Liberia: Past and Present of Africa's Oldest Republic. Accessed
2016. http://www.liberiapastandpresent.org/RitualKillings
1900_1950b.htm.

Downes, Jonathan. *Monster Hunter*. Woolsery, UK: CFZ Press,
2004.

Hallowell, Mike. "Cleadon BHM." *Still on the Track* (blog), December 10, 2009. http://forteanzoology.blogspot.com/2009/12
/mike-hallowell-cleadon-bhm.html.

———. "Is There a Hairy Humanoid in the Hills?" *Shields Gazette,*
March, 8, 2012. http://www.shieldsgazette
.com/news/offbeat/is-there-a-hairy-humanoid-in-the
-hills-1-4326022.

Harpur, Merrily. *Mystery Big Cats*. Loughborough, UK: Heart of
Albion Press, 2006.

Hay, Mark. "The Leopard Man Murders of Africa." *Modern Notion*,
November 21, 2014. http://modernnotion.com/leopard
-man-murders-africa/.

Hurt, Terry J. "Haldon Hills Pet Cemetery." Flickr. June 14, 2014.
https://www.flickr.com/photos/terry-and-nikon/14583561438.

Junge, Werner. *African Jungle Doctor*. London, UK: George G.
Harrap & Company Ltd., 1953.

O'Dwyer, F. G. "The White Man's Grave." *The Overseas Pensioner
Association Journal,* 54 (October 1987). The British Empire. Accessed 2016. http://www.britishempire.co.uk/article
/whitemansgrave.htm.

Remington, Xavier. "What is a Werecat?" *Ask Mystic Investigators*
(blog), September 29, 2012. http://mysticinvestigations.com
/paranormal/what-is-a-werecat/.

Swancer, Brent. "The Mystery of the Murderous Leopard Cult,"
Mysterious Universe (blog). February 24, 2016. http://mysterious
universe.org/2016/02/the-mystery-of-the-murderous-leopard
-cult/.

Chapter 9: Bigfoot and Mysterious Apes

Downes, Jonathan. *Island of Paradise*. Woolsery, UK: CFZ Press,
2008.

———. "Return of the Shug Monkey." *Still on the Track,* March 30,
2009. http://forteanzoology.blogspot.com/2009/03/return-of
-shug-monkey.html.

Hall, Jamie. "The Cryptid Zoo: Shug Monkey." The Cryptid Zoo.
2005. http://www.newanimal.org/shugmonkey.htm.

Halt, Charles I. "Unexplained Lights." Memorandum to US Air
Force, January 13, 1981.

Radford, Ben. *Tracking the Chupacabra: The Vampire Beast in Fact, Fiction and Folklore.* Albuquerque, NM: University of New Mexico Press, 2011.

Redfern, Nick. *Chupacabra Road Trip: In Search of the Elusive Beast.* Woodbury, MN: Llewellyn Publications, 2015.

———. Discussion of ghost lights and ancient sites presented at Texas Ghost Lights Conference, Austin, TX, June 11, 2005. http://www.anomalyarchives.org/oldevents/050611txghost-lightsconf.html.

Riggs, Rob. *In the Big Thicket: On the Trail of the Wild Man.* NY: Paraview Press, 2001.

Sears, Ernie. Letter to Nick Redfern. January 3, 2002.

"Shug Monkey." Mysterious Britain & Ireland. Accessed 2016. http://www.mysteriousbritain.co.uk/england/cambridgeshire/hauntings/shug-monkey.html.

Chapter 10: Dangerous Mimics

Colp, Harry D. *The Strangest Story Ever Told.* Petersburg, AK: Pilot Publishing, 1994. Electronic reproduction by Bigfoot Encounters. http://www.bigfootencounters.com/stories/harrycolp.htm.

EsoterX. "The Fearsome Alaskan Tlingit Kushtaka: If It's Not One Thing, It's an Otter." *EsoterX* (blog), January 9, 2013. https://esoterx.com/2013/01/09/the-fearsome-alaskan-tlingit-kushtaka-if-its-not-one-thing-its-an-otter/.

Gordon, Stan. *Silent Invasion: The Pennsylvania UFO-Bigfoot Casebook.* Greensburg, PA: Self-published, 2010.

Neilson, Tara. "Legends of the Kushtaka." *A Daughter of the Walrus* (blog), September 17, 2015. http://www.alaskaforreal.com/blog/kushtaka.

"Tall Creature Seen by Witness." Report #2396. Bigfoot Field Researchers Organization. June 28, 1999. http://www.bfro.net/GDB/show_report.asp?id=2396.

Waller, Dennis. *In Search of the Kushtaka, Alaska's Other Bigfoot: The Land-Otter Man of the Tlingit Indians.* CreateSpace Independent Publishing Platform, 2014.

"What Is Bigfoot?" Oregon Bigfoot. Accessed 2016. http://www.oregonbigfoot.com/what-is-bigfoot.php.

Chapter 11: Blinded by the Light

Matthews, Marcus. *Big Cats Loose in Britain.* Woolsery, UK: CFZ Press, 2007.

Redfern, Nick. "Creatures in the Crop Circles." *Mysterious Universe.* March 10, 2016. http://mysteriousuniverse.org/2016/03/creatures-in-the-crop-circles/.

Scott, J. W. "Flying Saucer Incident, Avebury, Wilts., September 4, 1962." Report to British Royal Air Force Provost and Security Services. Accessed at National Archives, Kew, UK.

Chapter 12: Fairies and the Little People

Alchin, Linda. "The Dryads." Accessed 2016. http://www.talesbeyondbelief.com/nymphs/dryads.htm.

"A Selkie Story." Education Scotland. Accessed 2016. http://archive.is/n0KKv2016.

"Dryades & Oreads (Dryades & Oreiades)." Theoi Project. Accessed 2016. http://www.theoi.com/Nymphe/Dryades.html.

Evans-Wentz, W. Y. *The Fairy-Faith in Celtic Countries.* Wayne, NJ: New Page Books, 2004.

Gifford, Elisabeth. "The Secret History Hidden in the Selkie Story." ElisabethGifford.com. May 3, 2014. http://www .elisabethgifford.com/blog/2014/5/3/the-secret-history -hidden-in-the-selkie-story.

Thomson, David. *The People of the Sea: A Journey in Search of the Seal Legend*. Edinburgh, Scotland: Canongate Classic, 1996.

Towrie, Sigurd. "The Selkie-folk." Orknyejar. Accessed 2016. http://www.orkneyjar.com/folklore/selkiefolk/.

Chapter 13: Aliens That Probably Aren't

"1953 Hunrath and Wilkinson Disappearance." UFO*BC. Accessed 2016. http://www.ufobc.ca/kinross/planeMishaps /hunrathAndWilkinson.html.

Angelucci, Orfeo. *The Secrets of the Saucers*. Amherst, WI: Amherst Press, 1955.

———. *Son of the Sun*. Camarillo, CA: DeVorss & Co., 1959.

"Karl Hunrath." Federal Bureau of Investigation file, 1953. Accessed at National Archives at College Park, MA, 2001.

Redfern, Nick. "Kidnapped by a Flying Saucer?" *Mysterious Universe*, April 6, 2012. http://mysteriousuniverse.org/2012/04 /kidnapped-by-a-flying-saucer/.

Shaw, Tristan. "The Two Men Who Went Missing Looking for a UFO." *Bizarre and Grotesque* (blog), July 19, 2015. https:// bizarreandgrotesque.com/2015/07/19/the-two-men-who -went-missing-looking-for-a-ufo/.

Chapter 14: The Most Dangerous Shapeshifters of All

Baring-Gould, Sabine. *The Book of Werewolves*. New York: Causeway Books, 1973.

Emspak, Jesse. "States of Matter: Plasma." *LiveScience,* May 5, 2016. http://www.livescience.com/54652-plasma.html.

Guiley, Rosemary Ellen. *The Djinn Connection*. Pensacola, FL: Visionary Living, Inc., 2013.

———. "FAQs about the Djinn." Djinn Universe. Accessed 2016. http://www.djinnuniverse.com/faqs-about-the-djinn.

———. "A Short Course on the Djinn." Djinn Universe. Accessed 2016. http://www.djinnuniverse.com /a-short-course-on-the-djinn.

Guiley, Rosemary Ellen, and Philip J. Imbrogno. *The Vengeful Djinn*. Woodbury, MN: Llewellyn Publications, 2011.

Hanon, Andrew. "Bus Beheading Similar to Windigo Phenomenon." Canoe.com. August 12, 2008. http://cnews.canoe.com/ CNEWS/Features/2008/08/11/6413481-sun.html.

———. "Evil spirit made man eat family." Canoe.com. August 12, 2008. http://cnews.canoe.com/CNEWS/WeirdNews/2008 /07/20/6213011-sun.html.

"Swift Runner." Murderpedia. Accessed 2016. http://murder pedia.org/male.R/r/runner-swift.htm.

Strom Walker, Joey. "Swift Runner." Gods-and-Monsters.com. Accessed 2016. http://www.gods-and-monsters.com/swift-runner .html.

Taylor, Troy. "The Wendigo: The North Woods of Minnesota." Ghosts of the Prairie. 2002. http://www.prairieghosts.com /wendigo.html.

"The Wendigo Legend." Gods-and-Monsters.com. Accessed 2016. http://www.gods-and-monsters.com/wendigo-legend.html.

Chapter 15: Lycanthropy: A Strange State of Mind

Albarelli, Jr., H. P. *A Terrible Mistake*. Walterville, OR: Trine Day LLC, 2009.

Bores, George, trans. "A true Discourse. Declaring the damnable life and death of one Stubbe Peeter. ..." London, 1590. Electronic reproduction by the University of Michigan. http://name.umdl.umich.edu/A13085.0001.001.

Eisler, Robert. *Man into Wolf: An Anthropological Interpretation of Sadism, Masochism, and Lycanthropy*. London, UK: Spring Books, 1948.

Godfrey, Linda. *Hunting the American Werewolf*. Madison, WI: Trails Books, 2006.

The Lycanthropologist. "Trials: The Damnable Life and Death of Peter Stubbe, 1589–90." *Werewolf Theory* (blog), May 15, 2012. http://werewolftheory.blogspot.com/2012/05/trials-damnable-life-and-death-of-peter.html.

Otten, Charlotte, F. *A Lycanthropy Reader: Werewolves in Western Culture*. Syracuse, NY: Syracuse University Press, 1986.

Chapter 16: Men in Black and Black-Eyed Children

Barker, Gray. *They Knew Too Much About Flying Saucers*. New York: University Books, 1956.

Bender, Albert K. *Flying Saucers and the Three Men*. New York: Paperback Library, 1968.

Weatherly, David. *The Black Eyed Children*. AZ: Leprechaun Press, 2012.

Chapter 17: The Native American Connection

"Battle of Palo Duro Canyon, Texas." *Trips into History* (blog), May 23, 2013. http://tripsintohistory.com/2013/05/23/battle -of-palo-duro-canyon-texas/.

Chiltoskey, Going Back, comp. *Myths, Legends, Superstitions of North American Indian Tribes: As Told by Students of Haskell Institute.* Cherokee, NC: Cherokee Publications, 1995.

Kelleher, Colm, and George Knapp. *Hunt for the Skinwalker: Science Confronts the Unexplained at a Remote Ranch in Utah.* New York: Paraview Pocket Books, 2005.

Madmadisonplantier. "Malicious Myths: The Were-Hyena." *In the Dark Air* (blog), October 26, 2015. https://inthedarkair.wordpress .com/2015/10/26/malicious-myths-the-were-hyena/.

Mourning Dove. *Coyote Stories.* Edited by Heister Dean Guie. Lincoln, NE: University of Nebraska Press, 1990.

O'Brien, Christopher. *Stalking the Tricksters: Shapeshifters, Skinwalkers, Dark Adepts and 2012.* Kempton, IL: Adventures Unlimited Press, 2009.

Redfern, Nick. *Chupacabra Road Trip: In Search of the Elusive Beast.* Woodbury, MN: Llewellyn Publications, 2015.

———. "Searching for California's Skinwalkers." *Mysterious Universe*, October 27, 2015. http://mysteriousuniverse.org /2015/10/searching-for-californias-skinwalkers/.

Chapter 18: The Eerie Owl Phenomenon

Clelland, Mike. *The Messengers: Owls, Synchronicity and the UFO Abductee.* Rochester, NY: Richard Dolan Press, 2015.

Downes, Jonathan. *The Owlman and Others.* Woolsery, UK: CFZ Press, 2006.

Fuller, John G. *The Interrupted Journey*. New York: The Dial Press, 1966.

Strieber, Whitley. *Communion*. New York: William Morrow, 1987.

Chapter 19: Blood-Sucking Shape-Changers

"Aswang." Real-Legends-and-Myths.com. Accessed 2016. http://www.read-legends-and-myths.com/aswang.html.

Azuma, Kentaro. "In Search of Aswang: A Ghost Story, Monster and Sorcerer in Philippine Society." Issue on "The Living and the Dead," *Kyoto Review of Southeast Asia* 12 (September 2012). https://kyotoreview.org/issue-12/in-search-of-aswang-a-ghost-story-monster-and-sorcerer-in-philippine-society/.

Dous777. "Aswang (Philippine Ghoul)." Last modified July 26, 2011. http://www.mythicalcreaturesguide.com/page/Aswang+(Philippine+Ghoul).

Melton, J. Gordon. *The Vampire Book: The Encyclopedia of the Undead*. Canton, MI: Visible Ink Press, 2011.

Polidori, John. *The Vampyre*. London: Henry Colburn, 1819. CreateSpace Independent Publishing Platform, 2012.

Wright, Dudley. *The Book of Vampires*. New York: Causeway Books, 1973.

Chapter 20: A Catalog of Creepy Critters

"Arizona Wilder." Age of Truth. Accessed 2016. http://ageoftruth.dk/arizona-wilder/.

Barker, Gray. *The Silver Bridge: The Classic Mothman Tale*. Clarksburg, WV: Saucerian Books, 1970.

BBC. "Diana murdered, Al Fayed claims." *BBC News,* February 18, 2008. http://news.bbc.co.uk/2/hi/uk/7250002.stm.

Beach Combing. "The Were-Hyenas of Ethiopia." *Beachcoming's Bizarre Blog,* June 26, 2011.http://www.strangehistory .net/2011/06/26/the-were-hyenas-of-ethiopia/.

Cartwright, Mark. "Quetzalcoatl." Ancient History Encyclopedia. August 1, 2013. http://www.ancient.eu/Quetzalcoatl/.

Crystal6. "Kitsune." Mythical Creatures Guide. June 1, 2012. http://www.mythicalcreaturesguide.com/page/Kitsune.

Encyclopaedia Britannica. s.v. "Quetzalcoatl." Online edition. Last modified April 16, 2015. https://www.britannica.com/topic/ Quetzalcóatl.

Frembgen, Jurgen W. "The Magicality of the Hyena: Beliefs and Practices in West and South Asia." *Asian Folklore Studies* 57 (1998): 331–44. https://nirc.nanzan-u.ac.jp/nfile/364.

Icke, David. *The Biggest Secret.* Maidstone, UK: David Icke Books, 1999.

———. "Reptilian Agenda." Accessed 2016. https://www .davidicke.com/category/271/reptilian-agenda.

Keel, John A. *The Mothman Prophecies.* New York: Tor Books, 1991.

"Kitsune: The Japanese Fox." Kitsune, Kumiho, Huli Jing, Fox: Fox Spirits in Asian and Asian Fox Spirits in the West. Accessed 2016. http://academia.issendai.com/fox-japanese.shtml.

Majendie, Paul. "Al-Fayed calls royals a 'Dracula Family.'" *Reuters,* February 18, 2008. http://uk.reuters.com/article/uk-britain-diana-idUKL1584299520080218.

Massey, Gerald. *The Natural Genesis.* London, UK: Williams & Norgate, 1883.

Sergent, Jr., Donnie, and Jeff Wamsley. *Mothman: The Facts Behind the Legend.* Point Pleasant, WV: Mothman Lives Publishing, 2002.

Zero, Keith. "Arizona Wilder: Revelations of a Mother Goddess."
    Reptiles: Fact or Fiction (blog), February 18, 2014. http://reptilian
    -facts.blogspot.com/2014/02/arizona-wilder-revelations
    -of-mother.html.

Acknowledgments

A very big "thank you!" goes out to all of the following: Everyone at Llewellyn Publications, particularly Amy Glaser, Kat Sanborn, Kathy Schneider, Donna Burch-Brown, Lauryn Heineman, and Kevin R. Brown. My literary agent, Lisa Hagan, for her hard work, enthusiasm, and friendship. And, of course, many thanks to everyone who generously shared their accounts of shapeshifting with me.

To Write to the Author

If you wish to contact the author or would like more information about this book, please write to the author in care of Llewellyn Worldwide Ltd. and we will forward your request. Both the author and publisher appreciate hearing from you and learning of your enjoyment of this book and how it has helped you. Llewellyn Worldwide Ltd. cannot guarantee that every letter written to the author can be answered, but all will be forwarded. Please write to:

Nick Redfern
℅ Llewellyn Worldwide
2143 Wooddale Drive
Woodbury, MN 55125-2989

Please enclose a self-addressed stamped envelope for reply,
or $1.00 to cover costs. If outside the U.S.A., enclose
an international postal reply coupon.

Many of Llewellyn's authors have websites with additional information and resources. For more information, please visit our website at http://www.llewellyn.com.

CHUPACABRA
ROAD TRIP

in search of the
elusive beast

Nick Redfern

Chupacabra Road Trip
In Search of the Elusive Beast
NICK REDFERN

In 1995, Puerto Rico was seized with mass hysteria over a new menace lurking in the rainforests, gruesomely killing livestock, leaving strange holes in their necks, and draining their bodies of blood. Described by eyewitnesses as a devilish creature three feet tall with spikes along its back and a mouth full of razor-sharp fangs, the strange animal was given the name chupacabra—Spanish for "goat-sucker."

Join noted monster hunter Nick Redfern and his spirited crew as they traverse the rugged backcountry of Puerto Rico, Mexico, and Texas investigating the continuing legacy of this fearsome beast. Whether he's interviewing locals, analyzing physical evidence, or sorting out the facts from the legends, Nick's journey into the realm of the chupacabra will make you wonder just what's out there lurking in the night.

978-0-7387-4448-3, 264 pp., 5 ¼ x 8   **$15.99**

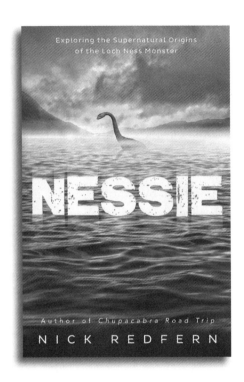

Exploring the Supernatural Origins
of the Loch Ness Monster

NESSIE

Author of Chupacabra Road Trip

NICK REDFERN

Nessie
Exploring the Supernatural Origins of the Loch Ness Monster
NICK REDFERN

Dive into the dark and turbulent domain of Nessie, the world's most supernatural monster.

Deep in the black waters of Loch Ness lurks a long-necked, hump-backed monster that for centuries has fascinated those lucky—or unlucky—enough to see it. From the earliest sightings in 565 AD to the Nessie craze of the twentieth century, this creature has been steeped in the world of supernatural strangeness.

Join Nick Redfern on an exciting journey into the paranormal origins of Nessie, exploring ideas that go far beyond the ordinary. This comprehensive guide offers lore, unique theories, hot spots, and photographs. Experience firsthand encounters, discover how Nessie is connected to the occult, and meet other mysterious monsters that live in Loch Ness. Nessie presents a fresh approach to the mystery, one that will take you down new and sometimes frightening paths as you hunt for the truth.

978-0-7387-4710-1, 264 pp., 5 ¼ x 8   **$15.99**

To order, call 1-877-NEW-WRLD or visit llewellyn.com
Prices subject to change without notice

A Menagerie of Mysterious Beasts
Encounters with Cryptid Creatures
KEN GERHARD

Draw back the curtain and marvel at the amazing collection of mysterious beasts within.

Join cryptozoologist Ken Gerhard on an enigmatic journey through the world of mysterious beasts, exploring eyewitness encounters with creatures thought to exist only in myths and legends. This compelling compendium presents a wide variety of astounding and bizarre creatures, from the Minnesota Iceman to the White Bluff Screamer to the Texas *T. rex*.

Discover the fascinating history and modern case studies of ape-men roaming the Americas. Experience captivating, first-hand accounts of dragon, werewolf, and mermaid sightings from Europe to Australia. Featuring sea monsters, colossal insects, enormous eagles, oversized amphibians, and more, *A Menagerie of Mysterious Beasts* is the ultimate resource for cryptid creature enthusiasts.

978-0-7387-4666-1, 240 pp., 5 ¼ x 8   **$15.99**
